Sunday Muddy Sunday

Pete May was born in 1959 in Bishop's Stortford. At Shenfield School in Essex his efforts for the First XI earnt him the nickname of Animal May. Since then his firm but fair performances have seen his peripatetic career encompass Bob Rule's five-a-side boys beneath the Westway, Philosophy Football, Shelter, Time Out, All Nations' Club, Stephen Brasher's five-a-side crew at Tottenham, and Conrad's team in red at Latimer Road. Like most Sunday performers, only a tragic lack of skill has kept him out of the FA Carling Premiership. He has been a freelance journalist for more than ten years and has written for the *Guardian, Independent, Time Out, Loaded, GQ, New Statesman* and *Goal.* He has a weekly column in *Midweek* and is a contributing editor of *FC.* His other publications include *The Lad Done Bad* for Penguin, written with Denis Campbell and Andrew Shields, and a contribution to the Sceptre anthology *The Agony and the Ecstasy.*

Sunday Muddy Sunday

The Heart and Soul of Sunday League Football

Pete May

First published in Great Britain in 1998 by
Virgin Publishing Ltd
Thames Wharf Studios
Rainville Road
London W6 9HT

A catalogue record for this book is available from the British Library.

ISBN 0 7535 0222 4

Typeset by TW Typesetting, Plymouth, Devon
Printed and bound in Great Britain by
Mackays of Chatham PLC

Contents

Acknowledgements

In 1993, Peter Freedman, the editor of *FC*, asked me to write a feature for a new FA magazine on grassroots football. Nothing would be the same again. It was the beginning of a meteoric dive into the muddy penalty area of Sunday-league football. Contacts and ideas from *FC* features have proved invaluable in the writing of *Sunday Muddy Sunday*, and everyone on the magazine deserves a massive thank you, including Peter Freedman, Tony Phillips, Adam Hay, David Cheal and publisher Michael Jacobs for his swift payments to an impoverished freelancer.

I'd also like to thank everyone connected with Sunday football for their help, but in particular David Lane of the Windy Millers, Joanne Griffiths and Stewart Cousins of the Flying Pig and George Ward of Milldean. And thanks to Ben Dunn, the Harry Redknapp of Virgin Publishing, for commissioning this book and ensuring there were (hopefully) no rickets, West Ham United FC for providing light entertainment and Irons in the soul, Rachel Cooke, Nick Toms, Nicola Baird for proofreading, advice, coffee making and tolerating life with a Sunday league anorak and our late cat Honey for seeing me through this work with her deskbound purring.

Finally, Sunday league football is by nature fluid, so by the time this book is published a few teams mentioned may well have disbanded to the public bar and some players will have retired, gone missing presumed shopping or been poached by rivals offering post-match jugs of beer. Have a good game.

London, March 1998

SUNDAY MUDDY SUNDAY

I can't believe the news today
Fifteen pints last night and we still have to play
How long, how long must we sing this song
How long? This morning we'll be lucky to score one
A mishit cross under the fat striker's feet
The late defender's Lada strewn across a dead-end street
But I will heed the battle call
Put my back up, my back up against the wall
Sunday muddy Sunday
Sunday muddy Sunday

And the battle's just begun
There's many lost but tell me who has won?
The trenches dug within our half
And mother's children, husbands, wives torn apart
Sunday muddy Sunday
Sunday muddy Sunday

(With apologies to U2)

Introduction

Who are the Men With Bags? Each Sunday morning they can be seen loitering on peaceful street corners, waiting to be bundled into the back of a juddering Lada or Transit van. The unenlightened citizen must be bemused. Are they churchgoers or male prostitutes? No, they are something altogether more perverse – Sunday league footballers.

Just what is in their bags has puzzled many great minds. Like Doctor Who's Tardis, the lads' bags are apparently bigger on the inside than out. Apart from uncleaned boots caked with dried mud and yellowing grass from last week, shin pads, lucky pants, a slightly soiled towel and an almost-empty bottle of shampoo, the bag might also contain a Snickers bar for breakfast and a bottle of Lucozade for rehydration purposes. The more intellectual performer carries several Sunday papers – although he's not as yet fit enough to get beyond the sports section – depositing a trail of advertising inserts along the pavement as his bag's zip is invariably undone or broken.

Were a Sunday league footballer ever to fall asleep on a glacier (not unknown on some pitches up north) and be frozen to death in the manner of Ötzi, the neolithic man discovered in the Alps, whoever found the player's body emerging from the ice 5,000 years later would have a perfect picture of Footballing Man in twentieth-century Britain. Right down to his amazing DIY hangover kit (aspirin, can of Stella and a copy of the *Sunday Sport*) and advanced medical technology (a can of Ralgex).

Sunday league football, like many of its participants, is massive. In the era of Premiership stars earning £20,000 a week, there are still tens of thousands of footballers all over the country who actually pay to play the game they love. There are roughly 45,000 registered clubs, usually fielding two or more sides. That means that each weekend there are approximately a million people playing football in England and Wales alone. To this total must be added all the footballers in Scotland and Northern Ireland and the legions of five-a-siders.

Many of the Premiership's more committed performers learnt to play in the Sunday leagues. Would Ian Wright celebrate his goals quite so enthusiastically if he hadn't started out as an unemployed apprentice plasterer playing for the Metal Box company team Ten-Em-Bee in the London and Kent Border League?

When Wrighty was on the bench for England, and Graham Taylor and Phil Neal were memorably captured by the TV cameras declaring, 'We'll get Wrighty on . . . We'll give Wrighty a go,' he must have thought he was back with Ten-Em-Bee. Sunday leaguers took heart all over the land. Despite the mystique of professionalism, those in charge had no more idea than the rest of us. If the lad turns up with his boots you give him a go and buy him a pint if he scores.

Other stars who've had to take their turn taking the kit down to the launderette for their Sunday side include Steve McManaman, Stuart Pearce, Chris Waddle, Jason McAteer, John Aldridge, Nigel Martyn, Peter Beardsley, Kevin Francis, Chris Armstrong, Dave Beasant and Steve Ogrizovic.

But, for most Sunday performers, professional status is only realised in their drunken dreams after they fall into a coma after ten pints. For them, football is the great male-bonding ritual.

Male footballers can forget all about the masculist movement that arrived from the US in the early 1990s, most significantly in Robert Bly's book, *Iron John*. There is no need for male bonding on wild-man tribal weekends for all those who know that Iron John was in fact a balding, beer-gutted defender, oblivious to head gashes and prone to running into the post without feeling pain. Clearly, Robert Bly has never known the ultimate wild-man experience, where, often for the first time in their lives, men learn to talk to each other honestly about their emotions, unleashing years of repressed pre-industrial tribal kinship in a primeval scream of, 'For fuck's sake, put 'im under!'

The bonding begins in the changing rooms. A bag is thrown on the floor and there's a rush for the kit that fits. The rest of the players are left with midriff-exposing shrunken shirts, bumster shorts and ankle socks. On occasion, the kit has been left unwashed and a collective chorus of abuse will be directed towards the miscreant responsible. Tactics are not as yet discussed. Instead, conversation centres on how many players are likely to turn up and a sober assessment of just how drunk the missing winger was last night before he was spotted walking across the top of the bar. For those who claim to be politically correct during the week, Sunday morning is a glorious all-male release, full of unsound banter about sexual encounters after the nightclub closed.

The pre-match build-up heightens as the sanctum of the dressing room is permeated with the smell of Ralgex and unwashed sweaty jockstraps. Studs clatter across cold, unforgiving concrete floors. Noxious fumes waft from the toilets – ten teams in the same changing rooms on top of all those Saturday-night excesses can have the most odious consequences.

An eccentric character known as the manager will then start behaving as if he's Kenny Dalglish or Alex Ferguson. With the dress sense of David Mellor merged with Tom Baker, he will come out with phrases like, 'This is the big one!', 'You've gotta want it today, lads!' and 'Remember to pick up the second-phase attackers!' His players will either grunt a vague acknowledgement or, as is more common, take the piss out of him.

Then, just before kick-off, the latecomers arrive. The prime directive of Sunday league football is that you can never be late just because your alarm failed to go off. To maintain any credibility, tardiness must always be the result of sexual or alcoholic over-indulgence. Latecomers will invariably mumble something like, 'Whoor, I had this forty-year-old last night!' or claim to have drunk fifteen pints, followed by a balti and a party that went on until 6.30 am. They will make a theatrical entrance five minutes after kick-off by running on to the pitch while still pulling on their shirts and doing up their sock-ties.

Often, your team will be at least two players short. Frantic Saturday, night phone calls from the captain or secretary will have resulted in excuses such as, 'I'm going shopping' or 'The groin strain's still playing up'. These will be followed by even more frantic Sunday-morning calls on the mobile pleading for 'ringers', mates who slept on the drunken striker's sofa last night, Harry Enfield's fat bloke from the pub and any hungover male capable of the slightest perambulation.

A typical game will start beneath skies the colour of Man. United's discarded grey kit with a team of nine players. After twenty minutes, your tenth man turns up, then, 0-4 down at half-time, your side illicitly recruits the bloke watching on the touchline, who proves to be your best player but then tells you that he can't play regularly as he normally goes to church on Sundays.

On the pitch, great skill – or, in some cases, any skill – is not required. The main prerequisite of the Sunday leaguer is to talk a good game. Football is full of quasi-masonic ritual: key words of great power to the initiated.

If a player can shout such phrases as 'Offside, ref!' whenever a goal is conceded, 'Have a word, ref!' after a dodgy tackle and 'Our ball!' whenever the ball goes into touch for a throw-in, then he is well on the way to acceptance from the footballing fraternity. When demanding the ball, a short, sharp phrase like 'Line!', 'Mine!' or 'Touch!' will sound professional.

A call that emphasises your tactical awareness and knowledge of the game will gain even more kudos with the lads. 'Man on!', 'Space!', 'Time!', 'In the hole!' or the Ruud Gullit-like 'Play it up the channels!' are all acceptable.

When a player is too knackered to run back, his simplest course of action is to moan at the rest of the defence, shouting phrases like 'Tighten up at the back!' and 'Sort it out!' with sufficient authority to deflect blame from himself. If a goal is conceded, players must cry either the aforementioned 'Offside, ref!', 'Lucky bastards!' or 'Who was on him?' Perhaps referees should abandon red and yellow cards and simply dispense green 'blame cards' to guilty defenders. It would save a lot of arguing.

Having conceded a goal, the player must then inspire the lads with a cry of, 'Come on, let's do 'em!' or, 'Another nine goals and we can still win this one!', which at least gets a laugh when your side is 8-0 down.

From the sidelines comes the constant shouting of rival managers, ranting instructions like, 'Remember the three Cs!', which noone ever can. The only other spectators are the subs (if they've got out of bed), a player's new girlfriend who hasn't as yet tired of watching her hero play, and the inevitable man with a dog. It would not be surprising to discover that Sunday league referees actually delay all kick-offs until the man with his canine companion appears. No one has ever encountered a game without this pair of foul-weather friends.

Astonishing transformations take place on the pitch. Sheepish accountants and civil servants suddenly turn into demented Vinny Jones-style psychos. Bricklayers become Fancy Dans. Fat blokes might even run for the first ten minutes.

Fitness is useful but not essential, although the ability to stand up does help. Sunday morning football is an equal-opportunities sport. Forget the chest trap. Beer guts are seen as an extra advantage in cushioning the ball (a technique known as the 'gut trap'), while baldness is a means of imparting spin on a glancing header.

And, even for the terminally unfit, there are plenty of rest periods. Throughout the game, the ball is constantly volleyed into the river or hoofed by over-zealous defenders on to a railway line or motorway. The manager of one sports ground where I played remained strangely unperturbed by numerous lost balls on the railway track. It later emerged he was sending the local kids to dice with the 125s to Cardiff in return for 50p – and at the same time probably drastically increasing the infant mortality rate in west London.

Entertainment and goals are guaranteed among the Sunday league stalwarts, for lack of skill creates far more chances than any combination of talent. Even the selection of linesmen is geared towards attractive play, the task normally falling to anyone foolish enough to turn up as a twelfth man or come off the field injured. The linesmen's ignorance of the offside law combined with the fact that most defenders are too slow to move forward at faster than walking pace has meant that the tedious offside trap has been all but eliminated from most leagues.

After the match comes the communal shower. Another of the immutable laws of Sunday football is that no shower has ever worked perfectly in the history of the game. Local authorities ensure that there are never more than five working showers and special controls make the water temperature veer between something like an Antarctic ice floe encountered by Sir Ranulph Fiennes and a hot geyser in New Zealand (the geyser effect is compounded by the mud pools resulting from the player who cleans his boots in the showers).

But queuing with towels and shampoo in hands, covered in mud and free from the restrictions of clothes, the lads return to the bonding process: ruminating about debatable penalties, outrageous referees and how the number nine got that love-bite.

The final stage of the ritual is the post-match pub analysis over beer (shandy is permissible during the first round as the player is, after all, an athlete), peanuts and crisps. The alcohol is to rectify any unnecessary weight loss and the conversation to convince yourself that your side was only robbed by a combination of inept refereeing, astonishing ill fortune and an unfair use of skill and pace by the opposition's strikers.

Not all the players who started the season will finish. It takes dedication and quite possibly a psychiatric condition to turn out on a bleak February morning after a run of seven successive defeats. But for those who play through their nine-month bad patch there is the reward of the end-of-season awards ceremony. Here, the bloke who wasted hours every week phoning 30 players and completing all the league formalities will be rewarded with a tacky £15 plastic-footballer trophy. A mounted backside will be presented to the player responsible for the miss of the season and the Slaphead of the Year Award will be a toothless comb which goes to the side's baldest player. And when it comes to survival of the fattest, the side's most corpulent player will receive a golden pair of scales.

The wealthier clubs might then embark on an end-of-season

tour, an experience that has brought terror to seaside towns throughout the UK and regions of France, Belgium and Holland. Here, the off-duty footballer perfects the art of being locked out of his boarding house at 3 am and failing to seduce the landlord's daughter.

The Sunday league experience is explored in full within the pages of this book. It is a tale of men behaving sadly; a trip into the heart of blokeishness that some will find enlightening, others amusing, and some plain frightening. But being juvenile is most of the point. The oldest wingers in town can forget about being responsible sales reps and indulge in true fantasy football each Sunday.

Some of the laddish behaviour might occasionally be construed as boorish but, in my travels searching the land for the ultimate game boys, football has seemed invariably a force for good. The lives of those involved are enriched by it, and dreams are nourished and friendships forged over pints and points. There is nothing quite like the hopeless male optimism of another scratch side hoping to avenge last week's 7-1 defeat. Even the role of the club programme writer and statistician proves that anoraks can be cared for in the community.

And another thing. Sunday league football is perhaps the last refuge of the British eccentric: the fat bloke from Aylesbury who thinks he's a Brazilian; the manager who wears stockings and suspenders beneath his day clothes; the goalkeeper poet who drinks a pint of beer between the sticks; the player who was clobbered in the face by the club mascot, a frozen monkfish; the midfielder called Captain Deep; the club fanatic who cleared a waterlogged pitch with a bucket and sponge; the side playing in Dennis the Menace shirts and wigs; and the supporter who urges his side on while clad in a Biggles helmet and giant pig's ears.

At the end of the day it promises to be a book of two halves – and don't be surprised if the final two chapters turn up twenty minutes late.

Sunday Muddy Sunday

1 It's a Funny Old Name

'And here's Des as the scores come through on the teleprinter.'
'We're just getting a result from the top game of the day: it's
Real Ale Madrid 2, Imaginary Madrid 1. Real Ale just edging
it in the Madrid derby there ... And how about this? A3 Milan
17, Norfolk Enchants 0. Norfolk Enchants really living up to
their name. Brixton Munchengladbach 3, Inter The Valley 1.
PSV Hangover 0, JCB Eindhoven 2. Dutch courage no use to
the home side there.

'And we're just hearing that the Windy Millers were winning
2-0 at home at their famous old Mile High Stadium when the
referee abandoned the game after the Windy Millers
participated in a collective Thunderbirds walk after the second
goal went in. Well, I wonder what Alan Hansen, or should I
say Captain Scarlet, will have to say about that on Match of the
Day *tonight? That's all from the teleprinter. Now it's over to*
James Alexander-Gordon with the classifieds.'

Even Paula Yates would be pushed to come up with sillier
names than most Sunday league sides. Never mind taking part
in a penalty shoot-out at the end of a World Cup semi-final –
the veterans of our bog-standard football realise that by far the
toughest thing in the game is coming up with a decent name for
your side.

A good name is essential to a team's identity and spirit. So
what's the secret of a good moniker? Many clubs turn to
continental sides for inspiration, giving them a local twist or
flavour. And when it comes to taking the pith, our Sunday
leaguers are world class.

The aptly named London Relegation League has contained

such sides as Brixton Munchengladbach, Inter The Valley (a side formed by a group of Charlton fans who presumably had a passing love of punk band The Skids), Who Dares Wednesday, Homerton Academicals and, best of all, Real Ale Madrid, a side worthy of sponsorship by CAMRA. As you'd expect from the names, there's a spirit of fun in the London Relegation League, whose motto is '*Aequi Simus, Juvenus*', or 'Let's Be Reasonable, Boys'.

Elsewhere are the likes of London sides A3 Milan (situated close to the A3 of course), JCB Eindhoven and PSV Hangover, not to mention Athletico Neasden. Other Big Smoke teams have included Red Star Belgravia, Charlton Aesthetic, Gotham City United and Racing Club de Blackheath. Barbarians FC were named after a particularly riotous tour of Malta in 1992.

Stupid names have been around almost as long as football itself. When the author was a student at Lancaster University, he was a proud member of a five-a-side team called the Morecambe Bay Rowdies. Younger fans should remember that the late 1970s saw Rodney Marsh and Pele turning out for the only slightly more skilled Tampa Bay Rowdies in the USA.

Like the best foreign films, some clubs' names have multi-layered levels of meaning. Take CK Bluventus from Orpington, Kent. The CK comes from Club Karaoke (the team's Saturday-night training), the 'Blu' from the Blue Anchor in which they drink, and the 'ventus' from the club's strip, which shares the black and white stripes of Juventus. South London side Milldean acquired their name by combining Millwall and Dean Martin. 'Most of the lads support Millwall and the original players were all a bunch of piss artists,' explains ex-secretary Barry Knox.

Five-a-side leagues throw up an ever-changing, organically growing mass of silly names, such as Gazza's Bellies in a Gateshead five-a-side league played in 1994 at the Pitz Super Soccer Complex (or should that be Pizza Super Soccer Complex?). Other league members included Borussia Munchenflapjack, Fat Thighed Monsters, Purple Battering Rams, Cheese On Toast and the marvellously named Norfolk Enchants (try saying it with a Geordie accent). A five-a-side team in Beccles,

Suffolk, were fishing around for a name and finally came up with Haddock Split after the Croatian side Hadjuk Split.

Sunday league clubs have even helped to thaw the Cold War. Brian Benson explains how Lokomotiv FC, surely a side of great pulling power, brought a whiff of eastern Europe to the playing fields of south London: 'Back in the mid-seventies our manager used to have exchange students from East Germany staying with him. As his son was leaving school and wanted to form a club, he decided to manage it. Some of the students had supported Lokomotiv Leipzig, so we took our name from that. Soon after we started, one of the lads wrote to Lokomotiv Leipzig in Berlin and they sent us an entire kit, which was a really great gesture. We still play in black and red stripes like Leipzig. And all this was before the Berlin Wall came down. You could say that we did our bit for glasnost.' Yes, the velvet revolution began in Croydon.

Other clubs like London side Perfidious Albion opt for the intellectual approach to a moniker. Only it seems they've played it too clever by half. 'Perfidious Albion was a Napoleonic insult aimed against England,' explains Albion's history man Hugh Jones. 'Not a lot of people get it. Come to think of it, I'm the only person who's ever really understood it.' Still, at least that Napoleon must make a good midfield general.

Then there's religious irony. Hendon Alternative Minyan played in the fourth division of the Maccabi (Southern) Football League. (Minyan is the minimum number required for a Jewish religious service.) 'I suppose that our initials of HAM were not that appropriate for a Jewish league,' said secretary Jeremy Kaufman. 'But then in 1994 we gained sponsorship from a local photographer called Chris Bacon and we changed our name to Ham and Bacon Sandwich.'

Other clubs' names are positively surreal, such as Imaginary Madrid in Manchester, Welsh side Rhyl Madrid and the FA Sunday Cup entrants Framwellgate Moor and Pity Me FC. Or, for that matter, Krakatoa FC, a side said to have the opposition literally quaking in their boots. If that isn't enough, there's also Bayern Banana, Inter Masala (an Asian side which never chickens out of 50/50 challenges), Slippy Fingers and Eccleshall Non-Political FC.

Then there was a Worcester five-a-side team called Where's Rupert?, named after senior player Bob Webb's sixteen-year-old son. Rupert turned up for a few games and was brilliant, before tiring of playing with a bunch of old gits. Weary of weekly cries of 'Where's Rupert?', the side decided to immortalise the fledgling who got away.

Occasionally, the players don't even know how the side got its name. The group of London players who took over the now-defunct West Coast Armadillos a decade ago had no idea how the club earnt its title, the origins of which are now sadly lost amid the annals of an old generation of Armadillos.

The Crouch End Vampires playing in the Southern Amateur League are not a team to gain a Terry Butcher-like head gash against. They are so named because their bleak ground by London's North Circular road overlooks a cemetery. Such an oppressive setting is said to be worth a goal – or should that be ghoul? – start to the home side, who will sweat blood for a result.

Other exotic names prove to have distinctly unexotic origins. Hasland Shoulder Of Mutton FC, for example, is not a team of psychotic butchers at all, but named after a pub. And what could have been the inspiration behind Hull side Deborah FC? A T Rex record? A biblical heroine? A sexual conquest? No, the club was actually named after its sponsors, a scaffolding company called Deborah Limited. The team has now changed sponsors and their new title is the more macho, if less romantic, B & A Scaffolding.

It's intriguing to think that Mick Lyons, the old Everton star, once played for Liverpool-based Lobster FC. The club's name has inspired plenty of 'Lobster Claw Back Result' headlines in the local papers, but again is no more than the name of a local pub.

The rise of women's football has allowed even more scope for imaginative names, none more so than London's Old Fallopians, conceived (arf arf) as a parody of public school old-boys' sides like the Old Harrovians. However, the killjoys at the Women's FA, attempting to ensure that women's football is taken more seriously, insisted that the Old Fallopians rename themselves the somewhat more prosaic Camberwell WFC for their games in the Greater London Regional Women's League. Still, the club's notepaper does still carry the Old Fallopians (founded 1990) letterhead, and to this day supporters cheer on the side with cries of 'Up the Tubes!'

Names of male sides tend to have baser origins. A five-a-side team in Bournemouth is called Amanda de Cadanet FC. It was formed specifically so that its members could say they'd scored with Amanda de Cadanet.

A name can be crucial to a team's collective psyche. The Windy Millers' name arose as an amalgamation of their former sponsors Mildon and the fact that they play at the Windmill Social Club, on top of a quarry known as the Windmill Mile High Stadium. Also in the mix is a character from the children's TV show *Camberwick Green*. Now the Nuneaton and District Sunday League side's goal-scoring celebrations centre around their moniker. 'When we score we all run round the pitch doing windmill actions and making high-pitched whistles. The other teams hate it,' says club supremo David Lane.

The club had originally wanted to be called Thunderbirds FC and to celebrate every goal with a collective Thunderbirds puppet walk, but the Brains at the county FA refused to allow the name, clearly unaware of the good work done by International Rescue.

A name has to be appropriate, though. Julian Clapton from Loughborough was fined £725 in court and banned for life by his league for punching a player about to take a penalty for Charnwood Forest against his side. Clapton had gone up to penalty taker David Stockwell and said that if he scored he wouldn't be walking home. Stockwell replied that he wouldn't be walking home anyway, as he had a car. Clapton then punched the penalty taker in the face, causing him to need three stitches to his lip. Unfortunately, the pugilist was playing for a side called the Old English Gentleman.

Individual county FAs can vary in their tolerance of silly names, even though David Barber of the FA says, 'As long as it's not offensive the FA would not step in and change a name.' So there's hope that A3 Milan, Borussia Munchenflapjack and PSV Hangover might yet grace the FA Carling Premiership.

Some Sunday league teams produce mottoes and club crests to go with their humorous names: an accurate crest for most Sunday league clubs might involve a pint of beer, a packet of fags, burger and fries, bog roll and lipstick stains. Whereas Arsenal have '*Victoria Concordia Crescit*' ('Victory Through Harmony'), Everton '*Nil Satis Nisi Optimum*' ('Only the Best is Good Enough') and Blackburn '*Arte et Labore*' ('Skill and Industry'), the Sunday league sides tend to go for a more 'Beerus Maximus' approach. One of the most innovative mottoes in the Sunday leagues comes from Good For The Game In General FC, based in Catford, London. Beneath the club crest of a commentator's mike and hat lie the words 'Always The Bridesmaidus Never The Bridicus'.

'We felt we needed a bit of Sunday league Latin,' explains director of football and just about everything else, Mick Pearce. 'I thought up the motto after we lost our first game 15-1, twelve years ago. Since then we've progressed to mediocrity. We did win a cup in a friendly league in 1989 but we've lost four semi-finals in five years, so the motto still holds true.'

Good For The Game In General's name is the result of a spanking defeat which was said to be, well, good for the game in general. Pearce says that other names considered by the club were the iconoclastic The Opposition's Crap FC and The Referee's A Bastard FC. Thankfully for the club's disciplinary record, these punk-style names were eventually shelved.

In Hertfordshire, Brookmans Park have a splendid-sounding motto in '*Exercitis Brookmans Cerritus*'. Is this some tribute to the health-giving effects of exercise? Er, no. 'It translates as Brookmans' Barmy Army,' explains secretary Jeff Spencer. 'It goes back to 1982 when we all used to sing, "We're the Brookmans' Barmy Army!" One of the lads went into the library and looked it up. It's on the club notepaper and pennants. A lot of the youngsters probably think it's a serious motto like "Who Dares Wins".'

Phil Colver of Colinthians (a parody of Corinthians) has also tried his best to introduce a team motto. 'I did think our motto should be "No Free Headers" or "Let's Have Quality", as one of our players shouts every time we get a free kick. Then I remembered that when I was at school we had a motto of *"Pulcher Im A Sequimina"* which means "In Pursuit Of Excellence". I put it above the teamsheet one week and they completely ignored it. We have a few Bosnian lads in the side and I think they thought *"Pulcher Im A Sequimina"* was just another player!'

And it's not just the amateurs who have a monopoly on dubious names. The *Guardian*'s Robert Pryce was once interviewing Robbie Fowler when the Liverpool striker revealed that he came from the Dingle and that his father was a top amateur player. 'I thought he must have meant Skelmersdale United,' says Pryce, 'but then I asked Robbie who his dad played for and he answered, "Valencia" – they were a Sunday league side!' Robbie's team-mate Steve McManaman also started off in the Sunday leagues, gaining his sea legs with Pacific.

There's also a guy works down the chip shop swears he's a Napoli star. Wrexham must have thought they'd got a bargain when they signed striker Karl Connolly from Napoli – until they discovered that Napoli was a Sunday league side formed by a group of mates in Prescot, Merseyside, and Connolly was working as a chip shoveller in a fish and chip shop. Karl's introduction to the pro game was the fantasy of every Sunday leaguer. At the end of a Napoli game, the referee called Connolly over. Connolly asked what he'd done. 'Nothing,' said the ref. 'I'm a scout for Wrexham and I'm going to recommend you for a trial.'

But who really wants professional football? If the best silly name the Premiership can come up with is Sheffield Wednesday or Tottenham Hotspur, then most players would prefer to stick with the likes of the London Relegation League. Only on the parks and pitches of Britain could you find a derby between Real Ale Madrid and Imaginary Madrid. All over the UK, teams like the Flying Pig, Windy Millers, Inter The Valley, JCB Eindhoven and PSV Hangover are competing, usually with Norfolk Enchants even if it is Good For The Game In General. Sunday league football: it's the Surreal Madrid.

2 The Usual Suspects

It's a fair bet that when Homo sapiens first took on a Neanderthal Man XI (rumoured to have been the original Wimbledon) 30,000 years ago, there was a player in the Homos' dressing cave taking the mickey out of the centre forward's new mammoth-skin coat and saying, 'Aye aye, lads, we'd better watch out this lot don't take their clubs out on the pitch with them.' And it's almost certain that there was a latecomer who ran on the pitch claiming that he'd been up all night hunting a sabre-toothed tiger.

Anyone doubting Richard Dawkins' theories about selfish genes would need only to observe the astonishing success with which the football gene has replicated itself among male humans. Men without the football gene died out through lack of mates, but those with the football gene drank lager and went forth and fornicated, passing on their football genes until they were dominant in their species.

Let us examine the manifestations of this genetic theory in practice. Inevitably, Sunday football has a high player turnover. Players can be transferred to opposition clubs, lured by a signing-on fee of two pints and the prospect of their kit actually being washed each week. Others will have gone missing presumed shopping or retired to spend more time with their satellite dish.

Youth-team players, too young to know about last season's abject record, are drafted in with the promise of being allowed to drink alcopops in the clubhouse without having to produce their driving licence. Fathers use emotional blackmail to coax their sons into appearing with a bunch of fat old gits. Experienced old pros are recruited from the public bar midway through the season. The centre forward's two mates might turn up as ringers, plus that bloke who was enlisted after being spotted walking his dog near the pitch last season. And the club psycho might suddenly return after serving a three-year suspension for punching a ref.

But be it in Newcastle, Manchester, Coventry or Yeovil, the same characters appear in every side with astonishing frequency. It's as if God has looked down and decreed that each side must have its Joker, Psycho, Veteran and Fat Keeper. Manwatcher Desmond Morris would recognise that beneath the subtle cultural differences (lager in London, Brown Ale in Newcastle), the male naked ape's physical and tribal needs are fulfilled superbly through the sport of football.

Here is a player-by-player analysis of a Sunday league side's main characters:

The Joker

Possibly a distant cousin of Gazza's and usually about as funny. He has nicknames for the entire squad by week one of pre-season training and loves to give a running commentary as he relieves himself of last night's vindaloo in the changing-room toilet. He enjoys farting in public, wearing false breasts, stealing players' clothes and placing a copy of *Fiesta* in happily married players' kitbags. The Joker believes he is vital to dressing-room morale and tries to lessen pre-match nerves by mimicking Harry Enfield characters ('Calm down, will ya!' 'Oi! Fat Keeper! No!'). When it's your birthday, the Joker will be the one who books the strippagram. If you have a Welsh player, he'll organise a whip-round for an inflatable plastic sheep at the end-of-season awards do. He likes to turn up for the last game of the season wearing either flip-flops, Bermuda shorts, a Hawaiian shirt and sunglasses, a Dennis the Menace wig or that perennial favourite, stockings and suspenders. Would be played in a movie by Martin Clunes.

The Bloodied Hero

Even in pre-season training, he plays on with bloodied knees from the bone-hard turf. He likes to think of himself as a latter-day Terry Butcher. Astroturf was a great invention for the Bloodied Hero. Festering burns are mere scratches to this man. And he doesn't think he's been in a game unless a clash of heads leaves a trail of blood trickling over his face. He's the sort of player who would run through a brick wall for the club and probably does when he's refused a drink on the club tour of Belgium. Heads anything that moves, even if the ball is only six inches off the ground. He loves to play on with a blood-soaked bandage around his head, looking rather like a concussed John Cleese in the classic *Fawlty Towers* 'Germans' episode. Even if he hasn't been injured, an old bloodied bandage applied at half-time usually psyches out the opposition. As he repels the opposition advances, he fantasises that he is defending Rorke's Drift in *Zulu* and would be played in a movie by Michael Caine.

The Veteran

He's still raging at the dying of the light (those floodlights were always crap) as well as at the ref. As long as anyone can remember, every season has been his last. The Vet has moved back through the side as the years have advanced and now uses his tactical acumen as a centre back in a partnership with a youngster who's only 35. They use their experience against nippy eighteen-year-old strikers – one pushes them and the other shoves them. He tends to get violent when team-mates ask him, in all seriousness, if he was in the Second World War. Since he discovered that Gordon Strachan extended his career by eating bananas, our hero has done the same, washing them down with three pints after the game. He's the butt of dressing-room jokes when he tries to be hip by claiming to like the Spice Girls but then confesses that he's never heard of the Prodigy or All Saints. In general, he ridicules all post-eighties music, which is why he still sports a Duran Duran tinted haircut. The Veteran refuses to listen to team talks as he says he's heard it all before. This mature star thinks of himself as the old head of the side and lectures younger players on the need for discipline on the pitch – although he still managed to hit one of his own players last season and is booked every week. Would be played in a movie by John Thaw.

Jekyll and Hyde

A quiet intellectual off the pitch. He buys Philosophy Football Camus and Wittgenstein T-shirts, reads the *Guardian*, is worried by gender stereotyping in *Loaded* and *FHM* and is happy to discuss – over a Diet coke – issues such as the role of Blair's New Labour in shaping New British politics. Yet on the field he's a complete nutter. He snaps like Roy Keane, scowls at linesmen and refs as if he were Bulgaria's Stoitchkov and hands out what that other left-wing intellectual, Vinny Jones, would refer to as 'a good clumping'. He's nearly always spoken to by the ref, can't resist verbals with opposition wingers, and is frequently booked or sent off. He storms off the pitch having been red carded, but as soon as he dons his day clothes, returns to being Clark Kent. Would be played in a movie by Jeremy Irons.

The Psycho

This man is so fired up for pre-season training that he inevitably ends up in a handbags-at-ten-paces confrontation in the first five-a-side. The side's Mad Dog models himself on Stuart Pearce, Julian Dicks and David Batty, although he thinks all three are a bit soft for his liking. He makes Begbie from *Trainspotting* seem phlegmatic. The Psycho likes to check if opposition players' suntans are fake or not by breaking their legs. He constantly abuses his team-mates for their lack of commitment, using what used to be quaintly termed as 'industrial language'. He even shouts at the bloke who was standing on the touchline but has been cajoled into turning out for the club as you only have nine players. Invariably, he has to be separated from opposition players at the final whistle. When sent off after unaccountably giving a slap to an opposition player, he is always quick to say at half-time, 'I'm sorry. I've let you down, lads. That was a stupid thing to do. Now let's get

stuck into these fucking bastards and give them a good kicking!'
Would be played in a movie by Dennis Hopper, Christopher
Walken or Robert Carlyle.

The Fat Keeper

The rotund custodian believes that if he carries on supping real
ale he'll eventually completely fill the nets. And strangely enough,
his team-mates go along with this theory. Like all keepers, he is
slightly eccentric, if not mad. He's as likely to punch the
opposition centre forward's head as the ball, which does mean he
tends to dominate his area. Models his dress sense on his hero
Neville Southall (who is a Sunday league keeper in everything bar
ability) and drives a battered Lada – its stop-start style mirrors
his sorties from his line. It's best not to give him a pink keeper's
shirt or the opposition might start calling him Mr Blobby. Never
lets his team forget the time he saved a penalty from a concussed,
partially sighted one-legged opposition centre forward. Would
be played in a movie by Robbie Coltrane.

Mr Fix-it

'Psst, wanna buy some CDs, mate?' Whatever you want, he'll
sell it to you over a post-match drink. When asked if he's
connected with HMV, he'll say that he's had the tests and he's
OK. This man has more contacts than Yellow Pages. He can
rustle up barbecue gear, an end-of-season disco and PA, a team
Transit and free sponsored half-time oranges before you've
finished a half of shandy. Obtains a knockout discount on the
team kit – even if it is a purple tartan or lime green. Not
particularly gifted on the pitch, but the manager daren't drop
him lest details of that box of adult videos he bought are
revealed. Would be played in a movie by Dennis Waterman.

Don Juan

Every Sunday morning he walks into the changing rooms
announcing, 'That bird weren't 'alf dirty last night!' His

conquests can range from grandmothers to sixteen-year-olds. The Don Juan never has average sex. He has always been seduced by a nymphomaniac with more sexual variations than even *Cosmopolitan* could include in its cover lines. Strangely enough, despite such a brilliant sex life, he never actually misses a game. Probably because he was in fact safely tucked up in bed the previous night watching *Match of the Day*, and his wife – to whom he's been completely faithful for ten years – insists he gets out of the house on a Sunday morning. Would be played in a movie by Neil Morrissey.

Diego Prima Donna

Blessed with great skill, in five-a-sides he beats players three times with fancy pull backs before passing back to his goalkeeper. This man is George Graham's nemesis. His team-mates soon discover that calling for the ball is pointless. Diego has an almost Cantona-like pride in his ability. To be substituted is a slight on his masculinity. He shrugs his shoulders in disbelief, curses the manager and has to be persuaded by his team-mates to leave the field. He refuses to join the after-match drink, complains solidly for the rest of the week that he should never have been substituted and threatens to leave the club. If he's subbed a second week running, he usually does. Would be played in a movie by Eric Cantona.

The Family Man

He's the one player who never showers and is off home to his missus within twenty seconds of the final whistle. His wife/girlfriend is a very reluctant football widow: every match he plays requires more negotiations and framework documents than the Ulster peace talks. His kit is often still muddy as she's refused to wash it and she has been known to sabotage his jockstraps with a pair of scissors. He's sometimes forced to bring his two young children and make them watch from the windswept touchline. His wife is rather like Mrs Mainwaring in *Dad's Army* – her presence is felt but she never actually appears, not even at the end-of-season awards ceremony. Would be played in a movie by Nick Berry from *Heartbeat*.

The Fashion Victim

There's always one player who believes himself to be a model pro. Catwalk variety, that is. The revival of 1970s fashions has caused a generation of youngsters to turn up for games looking like extras from *Starsky and Hutch*. Fired up by videos of Don Revie's England squads, the Fashion Victim's wardrobe includes flares, wide-collared shirts worn outside his jacket, a cheesy cardigan, full-length leather coat and George Best sideburns. This is doubly confusing for the older players, who are still wearing their original flared jeans from their Slade-supporting days. Sadly, the Fashion Victim is a flares player who often also plays like he's in a time warp. He thinks a good engine is a Ford Cortina, not something to be used on the football pitch. Would be played in a movie by David Soul.

Fancy Dan

The club's new signing displays bags of skill on the summer pitches. He has the wiry build of Steve McManaman and is so thin that he can't be used in a strong wind. He likes to think he's dancing with Wolves, but on winter Sundays he doesn't quite fancy mixing it with hungover defenders determined to kick anything that attempts a back-heel. He hates getting his shorts muddy and disappears during the game. The Fancy Dan starts taking weekend trips away and developing more groin strains than Darren 'Sicknote' Anderton. Somehow you know he won't be there in February. Would be played in a movie by Jane Horrocks.

The Gambler

The Stan Bowles of the Sunday league, he sneaks out without paying his subs and goes straight into the bookies. If by any chance he does have to pay his subs, he immediately tries to win back this unnecessary outlay. His form is directly affected by the previous day's Yankee or the 66-1 outsider at Kempton Park. He will bet on anything football related, from the game's first booking or throw-in to the size of the crowd (usually two). Never buys his round; instead tries to barter in dubious tips and 'dead certs'. Would be played in a movie by John Simm (Danny from *The Lakes*).

Shaggy

The team scruff. Like Steve McManaman, he models himself on Shaggy from *Scooby-Doo* and is never spotted with shampoo or a comb in the changing rooms. Takes endless stick from his team-mates and was once presented with a Happy Shopper bag as a tribute to his sartorial elegance. His ultimate fashion crime was to be seen in town on a Wednesday afternoon wearing the purple team shirt as leisurewear. On the field, he makes Steve Claridge and Ian Marshall look smart. His shirt is always outside his shorts and tie-ups are unheard of, leaving shin pads flopping over baggy socks. Would be played in a movie by Bob Geldof or, if an animated film, by Shaggy from *Scooby-Doo*.

The Latecomer

This geezer was almost included in the next chapter but has just sneaked in. He's the person you always see getting changed on the touchline when the game is fifteen minutes old and you're already 1-0 down, running on to the field without tie-ups or shin pads. He always strains a muscle because he hasn't warmed up properly. He has what Christian Gross might believe to be a particularly English attitude problem. Each Sunday morning his journey involves more unexpected detours than John Cleese in *Clockwise*. His ancient car doesn't go faster than 35 mph and he can only overtake driving downhill with a strong wind behind him. His car never starts in winter without jump leads and can almost invariably be guaranteed to stutter to a halt on the way to the game, causing a late sprint to the ground. He has the map-reading skills of Mark Thatcher. If he comes by bus you can guarantee he'll miss it, while his pushbike suffers from flat tyres and a loose chain. His excuses for being late are invariably pathetic. And he's always the last one to the bar. The only time he is ever early is the weekend when the clocks go back and he arrives 45 minutes before kick-off, pulling up his shorts and running for the pitch. Would be played in a movie by John Cleese.

The Secretary

The Secretary was once a player but has been persuaded by the rest of the team that he should move upstairs because of his phenomenal organisational skills. (But really because he's crap.) He has more diplomatic skills than Robin Cook, and is expert at explaining to a team that has travelled 30 miles for a game why his own side only has eight players. After the game, he can be found shuffling in his pockets trying to change a £20 note, while the rest of the side scarper. During the post-match drink he spends his time hunched over a table completing his match report, pinning the club prize-draw results to a noticeboard and compiling the latest league table and up-to-date appearance records for each player. He is permanently engaged in a Kafkaesque battle against authority, relishing battles with the various local FA committees over unjust suspensions and match postponements. By presenting him with a Clubman-of-the-Year award last season, the players have convinced the Secretary that he's an indispensable hero who does invaluable work behind the scenes. Even though they really think he's a sad bastard. Would be played in a movie by James Fleet (that wet bloke Hugo from *The Vicar of Dibley*).

3 The Six-Pint Fixture

The lad shimmies and feints through a crowd of bodies. He accelerates past pushes, shoves and attempts at obstruction and tolerates the vicious verbals. He ghosts into position and then, spotting an opening, he moves inside and hits the bar. 'Two pints of lager and a packet of crisps, please.' He's finally been served before last orders, he's on his sixth pint and the barmaid is looking more and more attractive, and our star's only worry is, will he ever make it on to the pitch for tomorrow morning's match?

William Shakespeare (whoever he played for) described the first of the seven ages of man thus: 'At first the infant, mewling and puking in the nurse's arms . . .' Sadly, most footballers don't get beyond that first age of man, especially on a Sunday morning. Isotonic drinks be buggered. Every weekend a nation of Sunday league boozers cope with that perennial problem: how do you play with a hangover? Or more importantly, how do you stop yourself throwing up over the referee? This dreadful state is familiar to most players: the sunlight is like a laser lacerating the cranium, the huge opposition striker resembles some drug-induced hallucinatory creature from a William Burroughs novel, and heading the ball is like connecting with a house brick.

Even God is aware of the role of lager in Irvine Welsh's short story, 'The Granton dropped, Granton's number 10 Boab Edinburgh pub, as you do after several pint 'You've goat the power tae cut doon oan th Nae buts aboot it. You've goat the power a mair positive contribution tae the Gran

Many top internationals have liked a drink or ten. Jimmy Greaves, Paul Merson and Tony Adams might now be rehabilitated figures, but sadly there is little expert counselling available to the stars of Sunday league sides – apart from their team-mates' advice to get the round in. There are no Arsène Wengers to insist on steamed broccoli and pasta for Christmas dinner and a single glass of wine on the eve of a big match. And even Delia Smith's new football recipes for sporting fitness have been shunned by teams favouring post-match roast potatoes and sausages with lager for dessert.

We've all been there – staggering out of bed on a Sunday morning as the manager's phone call deafens sensitive ears, desperately trying to rehydrate with Lucozade. But football is all about team spirits, and most Sunday league managers accept that a good booze-up is invariably good for camaraderie. And if they didn't, they'd probably have a pint of lager poured over their heads. 'Drinking together on a Saturday night and Sunday lunchtime keeps up morale, although we don't actually drink on the pitch,' says Melvyn McMahon of the meaty Chesterfield side Hasland Shoulder Of Mutton. 'Mind you, one of our lads remembers playing for a pub side who were a bit rough. They used to get a 21-pack out at half-time!'

At the Masons Arms in Yeovil, they love their pub games. 'We play skittles and a lot of the lads play in a pub skittles league. Then they turn up for football the next morning and play like skittles,' explains bowled-over secretary Martin Bester.

Such is the drinking culture of Sunday football that many clubs even report cases of footballers playing like their drinks. 'I've got a striker who's all fizz and no bottle,' admits John Wright, manager of the Wheatsheaf in Dudley. 'He snatches at everything.' At the Masons Arms in Yeovil, Martin Bester recalls a burly centre half called Fishy: 'We're in cider country and he drank rough scrumpy and he played like it. He'd kick anything that moved.'

For some, playing with a hangover is a way of life, their being finely attuned to performing the morning after the before. 'It doesn't make a great difference at our level,' Benson of Lokomotiv FC in south London. 'We always seem to play normally when we're all hungover. Even if we're still drunk, it doesn't seem to make any difference.

'A few years ago some of the lads turned up straight out of a nightclub and played no differently. The other week we had two lads phone up the manager at six in the morning, saying, "We're at Charing Cross. We've been to a nightclub. We can't play unless you pick us up." The manager said sod it, as he lived in East Grinstead. They did get there eventually. They didn't play but they made it into the pub.'

Benson does concede that actually vomiting on the pitch might affect your game. 'Some of the lads have been sick on the pitch or in the first-aid bucket. We've all done that, but if you've had a skinful the night before, it's worse not being there, as they're your mates and they'll let you know if you've let them down. So you turn up even if it means standing there white as a ghost and kicking the ball away every time it comes at you. You'll be there in body if not in mind.'

Most sides would surely concur with Tom Waits when he sings in his ravaged voice that 'the piano has been drinking, not me'. Mick Pearce of London side Good For The Game In General recalls his goalkeeper trying a hair of the dog. 'He had a can of lager the morning after and kept a clean sheet. He just stopped everything they threw at him and he was full of himself. So the next game he tried something even stronger – a can of Tennant's – and we were 3-0 down at half-time. He never tried that one again.'

But there are enough unexplained cases of hungover teams playing better than normal to baffle even Carol Vorderman. The Flying Pig's Stewart Cousins has a radical hangover cure: 'Keep drinking so you don't get one!' The Cambridge side had just won a cup tie despite over-indulging at t̶ ̶ ̶'̶s̶ wife's 30th birthday party the night before.

'A lot of the players had huge hangovers, ̶ two and we beat a division one side 3-1 aw̶ a couple of years ago, the manager put us u̶ got stuffed. We were all at the party in̶ turned up in the morning still wearing ou̶ nurse, one of the centre halves was a B̶

Batman and Robin, and a thieving Scouser. I think that psyched the opposition out a bit. After the game we had a few more beers in their pub and watched the footie on TV.'

Andy Taylor of the New Inn Sidley in Sussex remembers a famous cup tie in 1994. 'It was our landlord's wedding anniversary and we were finally kicked out of the pub at 2 am. We had a crucial cup tie in the morning and we were brilliant. We drew 2-2. Then we all went to bed early for the replay and we got walloped!'

But more often than not, hangovers inevitably affect performance. The wedding of the Alma Tavern's centre half resulted in them losing the Middlesex County FA Cup Final against West Hendon. 'Our centre half had been married the day before so we were all a bit worse for wear,' reveals secretary Andrew Nicholls. 'We'd arranged for a strippagram to come into our dressing room before the match but she went into the opposition's dressing room instead – leaving us to pick up the bill!' Talk about giving the opposition a goal start . . .

Nicholls continues his cautionary tale. 'Soon after kick-off, our hungover and newly married centre half gifted them a goal. Then our goalkeeper broke his hand and we replaced him with our centre forward. We recovered to score two goals, but then the centre half gave away a penalty and our replacement keeper gave away another goal by dropping a tame shot.' The only consolation for the defeated Alma Tavern lads was that at least the centre half had chosen to spend his first day of nuptial bliss playing football instead of doing anything so silly as going on honeymoon.

One of the most bizarre goals ever seen in football was witnessed by Nick Toms, playing for a Labour Party side against ASLEF. 'It was just an innocuous punt upfield but the ball went straight into the net. The goalkeeper was in the back of the net throwing up! We were all laughing and the poor keeper was just getting abuse from his team-mates.'

Other players are so hungover they need a drink. Luckily, one tion George Best never had to cope with was actually in the pub itself. Like Bestie, many Sunday league succumbed to the pressures of non-superstar status and low fan expectations and taken to the sauce. 'I had one lad called Kevin who wouldn't play without a drink,' remembers Keith Lee of Cheshire side White Hart Hyde. 'We'd change in the pub for a 10.15 kick-off and he'd ask the landlord to pour him a drink! Mind you, he threw up once and I had to rub it into the mud to make sure the ref didn't see.'

Half-time, gentlemen, please! Tales of interval boozing abound. 'We played a side once and there was a hell of a row in their dressing room at half-time,' remembers Andy Taylor of the New Inn Sidley. 'They worked on the ferries and they were opening up cans of Stella. They were all over the place in the second half.'

In Wandsworth, south London, drinking – not football, it seems – is more important than life and death. Mike Pattenden of Millbank recalls a bizarre cup final: 'We were in the final and set to play this pub side from Wandsworth who were renowned for being horrible thugs. Then the cup final was turned into a memorial game for their goalkeeper, who a week earlier had been beaten to death with a baseball bat.

'We thought it was looking a little dodgy when a double-decker bus full of their fans turned up at 11.30 in the morning and they were already boozing. The game wasn't too bad at first. But on the touchline the fans were drinking more and more as the bar had opened in the clubhouse. Their fans were all bringing out their pints of beer on to the touchline. The score was 1-1 when I beat the offside trap and slotted it past the keeper. The supporters had been giving the linesman, who was also the league secretary, a bit of stick before, but then they really started haranguing him, as they were adamant I was offside.

'Then someone threw a pint over him. The players joined in, pushing and shoving, and there were supporters and general mayhem. The referee abandoned the minutes to go due to crowd trouble, wit standing. The dead bloke's parents were th all ended in farce. I'd scored both goals in been abandoned ten minutes early. The m in a slightly tense atmosphere and some contrite, as they should have been. They were kicked out of the league after that.'

And of course the drinking starts all over again once the match is over. The sensible athlete would rehydrate with water or fruit juice, but sensible players don't turn out for their pub side. Players in the Premiership might be on a-grand-a-goal bonuses, but pub sides have their own unique after-match incentive schemes.

'The landlord said he'd give one of our players a pint a goal,' says Darren Murphy of the Ship Inn in Wirral, Merseyside. 'His strike rate certainly improved and he ended up costing the pub quite a few beers. In fact, we beat one side 14-0 and 11-0 home and away and he ended up with about eight free pints.'

At the New Inn Sidley they have an even more enticing bonus scheme. 'The landlord gives us a four-pint jug of beer for scoring a hat-trick, saving a penalty or winning a man of the match award,' reveals Andy Taylor. 'I scored two hat-tricks in one game but I couldn't drink eight pints so I had to share my award.'

As well as jugs brimming with ale, the New Inn's general ambience also helps to lure new signings, claims Taylor. 'The landlord does barbecues after the game and a meat raffle every week. Plus we've got Sky so that definitely helps us recruit new players.' Who needs Eric Hall when a meat raffle is the only signing-on fee necessary?

The sick men of football

But when it comes to pre-match drinking, perhaps the sickest men in football are south London side Milldean, a team whose knowledge of hangovers would shame even Oliver Reed. 'In the early days we hadn't had a night out unless there were a couple of blokes puking behind the goal,' laughs secretary George Ward. Nowadays, he doesn't mind his players having a drink, ~~t~~ he does expect them to be able to stand up on the pitch.

~~e~~ other week, two young players threw up at half-time. I ~~b~~oots with me just in case anyone was injured. But they ~~m~~e on and I had to say, "I've been at work all day.

I'm not coming on if they can't handle their beer!" We pushed them back on and they just died in the centre circle.'

As a player with Milldean, Ward saw so much bile he must have imagined he was in a remake of *The Exorcist*. 'Once an opposition captain was standing at the centre spot waiting to kick off. He just said, "Hang on a minute, ref" then threw up, and as cool as you like continued, "It's OK, ref, you can kick off now." The ref went mad and made him get a bucket to clear it up. On another occasion, our manager was giving his team talk and this bloke was throwing up. It was real yellow bile and we all felt like throwing up too. We didn't remember a word of that team talk. That's the thing about throwing up; once one player does it everybody else wants to do it too.'

And we thought Gazza had refuelling problems. Ward continues: 'Before one match one of our players let out a disgusting fart in the changing room. Another player said, "Yeugh, I can taste it!" and the next minute he was sick. We had a bloke throw up in the showers after one match. It was all going down the drain and this gang of big hairy blokes were all jumping out of the way.'

Even Milldean match officials have been affected by the Sunday morning post-binge nightmare. 'We had a linesman throw up once,' continues Ward. 'We called for offside and were wondering why the flag hadn't gone up. Then we looked at the linesman and he was throwing up. We were all saying, "We're sick of your decisions too." You get no sympathy in football at all if you throw up.'

With all this experience of regurgitation, the Milldean man seems the natural candidate to ask for tips on playing with a hangover. 'Running it off is the only cure,' Ward says confidently. 'If you throw up or faint it's going to be in the first fifteen minutes. If you're still standing up after fifteen minutes you'll get over it. But once you start throwing up yo⌐ stop.'

For further evidence of the drinking culture, you ⌐ visit Hackney Marshes at ten o'clock on a Sunda⌐ groups of men with bags mingle by the changin⌐ uncommon to see players eating burgers and⌐

lager. Sightings have included a player and his girlfriend, surrounded by kids, standing by their battered car drinking cans of lager and 'avin' a fag before kick-off, looking suspiciously like Wayne and Waynetta Slob.

One former player tells of a Marshes goalkeeper who used to park his motorbike behind the goal and then take periodic swigs from a flagon of beer in his helmet box. 'The groundsmen would go mad when he just drove on to the pitches. Mind you, with all that drinking he was pretty rubbish.'

Amid all the fuss Newcastle made about playing at Stevenage in a fourth-round FA Cup tie in 1998, it was at one point suggested by Newcastle that they'd play Stevenage on Hackney Marshes if necessary. And it might have been better, and certainly more amusing, if Stevenage had insisted on playing at the Marshes. The thought of Stuart Pearce being told to turn off his ghetto blaster by a council jobsworth, Kenny Dalglish trying to stop Alan Shearer downing a can of Tennant's and Keith Gillespie tucking into a burger before kick-off is simply irresistible.

At Hackney Marshes they even carry on drinking in hospital. Rachel Savage, a former nurse at Homerton Hospital, remembers players coming in who were more concerned to find out the final score than details of their injury:

'They'd arrive in casualty or orthopaedic wards complaining about missing the game and still wearing their skimpy shorts and stripy socks and they were always covered in mud,' recalls the former angel. 'Often they'd be accompanied by a girlfriend who was more concerned about their broken leg and would be telling the player that he's too old and unfit and should have taken up a safer hobby. Usually the girlfriend would disappear when their wife appeared.'

But injured players are not forgotten or ignored as they sometimes are at professional level. Their fellow performers would arrive to provide counselling – and besides, it made a change from the pub. Casualty would become even more ~~tous~~ than usual when the rest of the squad arrived straight ~~the~~ showers.

~~replace the pub with the hospital and discuss the finer~~

points of the game, try to chat up the nurses, and discuss next week's tactics,' says Savage. 'I'd also catch them trying to slip a can to their injured team-mate for 'pain control'.

'But if a tetanus shot was required, it would usually stop their bravado when you told them to drop their trousers not roll up their sleeve! In general, the footballers were quite good-natured, although occasionally a porter or two has had to evict them from casualty when the songs started.'

Even a broken leg or arm can't stop the Sunday league footballer turning to drink. He thinks a six-pack stomach is achieved by drinking just that amount every night. Many players do indeed have a drinking problem – and it's how to get served as quickly as possible after the game.

4 The Crazy Gang

Saturday night. Nuneaton is full of eighteen-year-old girls in frighteningly short mini-skirts wearing knee-length boots and no tights in winter. This is the Windy Millers' pre-match preparation on a Saturday night – exploring the fleshpots of Nuneaton. Alex 'Taggart' Ferguson would become even redder in the face and quite possibly spontaneously combust if he were ever to witness such scenes.

First off we're into the Pen and Wig, which is a pub full of loud music and blokes in button-down shirts worn without jackets. Windy Millers supremo David Lane, an ageing New Romantic now working as a sales rep for a national freight company, introduces some of the lads. 'We've got more characters than Harry Enfield,' he says.

At the bar are McVey (he apparently has no first name although it's rumoured to be Richard), who is wearing a bad taste spotted orange beach shirt from a club tour, John 'Donkey' Cole (another founder of the club), The Reject (a player who left for a rival club) and Tel (club secretary/first-team manager Paul Kettell).

David Lane is the self-titled director of football and Alex Ferguson-like supremo. Only, whereas Ferguson is nicknamed 'Taggart' by his charges, the Windy Millers refer to their club patriarch as either 'Laney' or the less respectful 'Fat Lane'. At 38, he admits to being slightly over his ideal playing weight.

For David, the secret of a successful club lies in social activities. 'We go for the rugby club spirit more. We always have little groups, such as the Rent Shop Boys (our sixteen-to-eighteen-year-olds) and the finance committee, that meet throughout the season. We produce our own fanzine, bet on results, and we have club nights out and go to Zapzones (games with laser guns). You can have the best bunch of players but you've got to have that club morale as well.' And the Windy Millers are nothing if not social.

After a swift round it's on to another theme pub called Bilberries. On the way we meet Adam, a youngster who's moving to the West Country. 'I'll get that tour in Exeter organised,' he tells Laney. Adam is known as Glass Back to the rest of the squad 'because every time he gets an injury he's out for a week'.

It seems that Lane knows everyone in Nuneaton, judging by the numerous greetings he receives in the street. 'It's all through the football, really. Everyone's played for us at some point,' he explains.

The lads opt for more pints of lager and bottles of Rolling Rock. 'Captain Deep!' holler the Windy Millers contingent, spotting former midfield legend Captain Deep across the bar. 'None of us could ever understand him,' explains Lane. Captain Deep is apparently pleasant and smiles a lot, but he has another, darker, side.

'He has these deep moods and he's very intense, but as we're a bunch of piss artists we've got no worries with Captain Deep around because he's an expert in martial arts,' explains Laney. 'He's a bit of a superstar. When he used to play for us he was worth three goals a game.'

Glass Back joins us and announces with Eubank-like confidence: 'I'm the best player. I used to play semi-pro but I've been injured. The doctor said I could never play again, but I'm still giving it a go. I'll chance it tomorrow as it's my last game.'

Glass Back is a lad with recovery powers worthy of Jesus and is determined to turn out for his final match in the morning – although as this is his leaving party he's not sparing on the beer.

'What's Laney like as a player?' I ask Glass-Back.

'Laney isn't bad, but he's a fat bastard now.'

'It's Billy!' shout the Millers posse. He's also known as Scuff because he scuffs the ball. 'His missus will kill him.' Another ex-star has been spotted, chatting up a young reveller in a mini-skirt. 'Quick, has anyone got a condom?' asks McVey.

The lads search through their wallets and someone produces one. After some exaggerated waving at Billy, McVey walks over and hands it to him.

We move on to Chico's, a heaving disco/bar, and a few pints later head for a nightclub, Millennium, following Billy and associate. There's a huge queue and unfortunately for Billy we're standing behind him and his new female friend. They receive yet more stick. Playing with the Windy Millers must do nothing for your love life. Two, ahem, robust Nuneaton babes are standing behind us. 'Are you wearing that shirt for a bet?' they ask McVey.

'I am, actually! It's nice, isn't it?' The shirt is a leftover from the infamous Windy Millers tour of Whitley Bay when the lads invaded the town dressed in orange.

The women get chatting to the lads. 'It's so cold my nipples have got nipples,' says one. David Lane's blond hair is receiving particular attention. 'Oooh, his hair's so soft. What do you use? It's Marc Almond!' Lane's Windy Millers team-mates instantly break into a terrace chorus of Soft Cell's 'Tainted Love'.

One of the lads then tries the classic chat-up line. 'Have your knickers got a mirror on them? Because I can see myself in them.' The girls chortle.

At last we enter the bowels of the club. Inside, it's a mass of peroxide, teeth and glowing bras exposed under strobe lights. The lads pile to the bar, shouting conversations at each other. There are go-go girls dancing in cages. The whole of Nuneaton seems to be going mental.

By midnight, David Lane, who's driving and drinking only Coke, is a little worried about some of his players. 'We need Tel tomorrow to keep the others going in midfield. They're all a bit young. Tel gets stuck in and gees them up when things aren't going well. I can tell when he's gone past the point of no return. He's supposed to be marking the pitch at seven tomorrow morning.'

At 12.30, with the team showing no signs of stopping drinking, Laney drives me back to my hotel. In the car, as we veer past staggering revellers, Lane starts to bare his soul. (No, lads, I said soul.) 'I'm thinking of knocking it on the head soon.

We've got some good young players and some good old ones, but nothing in between. Once the three of us who started it – Tel, John and myself – go, that'll probably be it.' He drops me at the hotel and returns to Millennium in a damage limitation exercise to try to ensure his charges are almost sober in the morning.

Sunday morning. It's difficult enough to get out of bed at 7.30, and I'm not even playing. At 8.30, Lane drives up to the Beefeater Hotel in his Audi. 'Tel's been coughing up blood and he was meant to be marking the pitch. His missus won't talk to him.' We pick up another young player and drive past McDonald's. 'Normally I have to fetch half of them out of there where they're having breakfast.'

On top of a windy hill overlooking a bleak quarry, lies the Windmill social club and next to it a neat-looking pitch, constructed by Lane and Co. back in 1986. It has to be mown with industrial lawnmowers in the close season and is generally cherished with more love than some of the Windy Millers womenfolk receive. Lane once painted the lines with lime-green emulsion by car headlights in the dark. 'Sadly they were all over the place when we saw them in the morning.'

On another occasion, this time a Saturday morning, Lane drove his car on to the pitch to inspect the lines. 'It was pouring with rain and then I discovered that my car was stuck! It was eight hours before I could get it off. I put my coat and sticks under it, but it still wouldn't move. I was in my suit, covered in mud, and the missus thought I'd left her as I said I'd be back to go out shopping in half an hour. I had to call the AA in the end and I wasn't off until seven at night.'

The players are arriving in the car park. 'We call this the Mile High Stadium,' Laney says with a proprietary air. At the end of the pitch lies a ditch that has often claimed unsuspecting forwards who've found slide tackles near the goal line have resulted in a fall into a trench from the First World War.

The Windmill clubhouse is an inviting building, but unfortunately the new committee won't allow the Windy Millers to change in it. The side's new home is a 40-foot container, obtained by Tel, who works in the building trade. 'Six people nearly died moving it,' laughs Lane. It's like a huge, windowless coffin, but is lit by fluorescent tubing. There's a small section for the away team and then a door opening on to a larger section for the home side. Next season the club plans to have framed shirts from past seasons on the walls, including the legendary tartan kit.

'THIS IS MANCETTER ROAD' reads an intimidating sign on the home dressing-room door. It continues: 'WINDY MILLERS ESTABLISHED 1986.' As the old footballing cliché goes, many teams must be beaten before they kick off. The home dressing room also has a sign up indicating that brave referees can change with the Millers. It says: 'Referee – is he blind?'

Tel is wearing acid-house trousers and looking rough as he cranks up the club generator. 'My head's a boomer. I won't want to be heading it today.' Eleven of the famous orange and black shirts are neatly hanging on the home team's pegs. Tel might be hungover but he knows his kit responsibilities can't be shirked. 'We've replaced our toxic-green kit with Tango orange,' he explains proudly.

On the club noticeboard is a picture of a naked McVey lying on a bed. Other naked snaps include Shaggy on tour and retired player Richard, who was not best pleased when the same picture was faxed to the bank where he works. Naked Windy Millers are not exactly what you want to see in the morning after a lager frenzy in Millennium, and the container could quite possibly be closed under the Obscene Publications Act. In contrast, the away dressing room is designed to intimidate in subtle ways: it has only a naked bulb and ten hooks instead of eleven.

In the car park, the lads are still assembling. There's Shaggy, the Beast and Mr Nice. Goalkeeper Keith 'Fashion Flaw' Jones arrives wearing a Sunderland shirt and flared jeans, but it's not retro chic – he looks like he's been wearing them continuously since the seventies. With his long black hair, he looks the double of Slade drummer Don Powell.

He has been known to dress worse. When he arrived for his

Windy Millers debut he was wearing a pair of flared jeans with bells attached. 'Nobody would walk with me because the bells jangled in the wind.' Keith then goes into an imitation of Mr Nice. 'He's the nicest man in football. "Please don't book him, Mr Referee. He didn't mean to foul me." '

Fat Lane leaves to captain the reserves, his car boot packed with footballs and kit. The lads begin to put the nets up as Keith tells me about a famous tour of Holland.

In the dressing container, Tel rings a huge bell that's hanging above the door, shouting, 'Wakey! Wakey!' It's a vital game in the Mitchells and Butler Nuneaton and District Sunday League against the old enemy Bridges. One of the lads is being tackled about last night's sexploits. 'Who was the lucky babe? Here, what's that trickling down your chin?' The players begin to change and attention centres on the team ghetto blaster. 'Gary Glitter's fucked,' says Tel, meddling with a tape.

Keith puts on 'Welcome To The Jungle' by Guns 'N' Roses at full volume and begins playing air guitar with a fag in his mouth. He's wearing pink socks, luminous green shorts, a horrendous dayglo keeper's shirt and a bizarre, multi-coloured cap that would not be out of place on the set of *Teletubbies*. Eventually Mel Smith (aka the Beast) thumps the stop button. Tel moves in with his resurrected Gary Glitter tape. 'Hello, hello, good to be back, good to be back . . .' The players are punching the air and chanting as the bemused 50-something referee comes in to change. 'All right ref? Have a chant!' someone hollers. The ref smiles nervously.

Eventually the ghetto blaster is turned off and Tel stands up and assumes a posture of extreme gravitas. 'Right, listen now, lads. Last week's result wasn't a reflection of the game. Seriously, we were a bit lax throughout the side. We must punish teams like that. It's got to improve. Listen, shut up . . . I want plenty of talk and no backchat to the referee. Everybody be vocal – except me. Right, let's do the stomp!'

The players huddle in a circle and stamp their feet, accompanied by the deafening tones of Gary Glitter. 'Come on, ref, do the stomp!' they exhort, but he declines their offer. The opposition, aware of the psychological warfare in the Windy

Millers container, have wisely opted to get changed in their cars.

The players are warming up. 'Who did those lines? They're crooked!' exclaims McVey, looking at a distinctly wobbly touchline.

'It was after a few pints,' explains Tel.

The game kicks off in front of a single-figure gate. The Windy Millers are being watched by McVey, recovering from a long-term injury, his brother, substitute Glass Back and the girlfriend of one of the younger players. 'Fifteen drinks for ten pounds can't be bad,' muses Glass Back, still reflecting on last night's result at Millennium. He's still full of confidence. 'I'm the best player. I've played semi-pro. It's my final match. Watch me – I'll go on and get a goal.'

'We had to fend off these fat birds,' says McVey, 'and then I fell for the dodgy chicken burger on the way home.'

On the pitch it's immediately apparent that Keith 'Fashion Flaw' Jones might look like a care in the community patient in his pink socks, green shorts and technicolour Rubettes cap, but he takes the game extremely seriously, producing a good early save and continually bawling out his defence. 'This ain't good enough. Let's raise it, Windmill!' It's also apparent that centre back Beast/Mel Smith can't even escape his nickname on the pitch, as Keith bawls, 'You've left a hole, Mel!'

Bridges are on top and take the lead. Midway through the first half, it gets worse. Tel swings his arm at an opponent and the ref has no choice but to send him off. Keith is incensed in his goal. 'What did we say, lads? What did we say?'

Tel comes off the pitch kicking the ground in frustration but still encouraging the lads: 'Come on, you Tangos! Movement!'

Half-time arrives with the Millers' ten men still only one goal down. They huddle together on the touchline.

'I'm sorry. I've let you down,' Tel says to the lads.

'It was a good slap. You didn't miss his head!' consoles a team-mate.

'We're not getting the second ball,' continues Tel. 'We're not up there quick enough. We've got to capitalise on the free kicks and corners. We can beat them for pace at the back.'

Keith takes over. 'It's unlike you to do that, Tel. Keep your head up, son. We're not out of this by a long shot. We've got to plug this gap in the middle at the back. Come on! You're fucking better than them!'

Tel makes a late tactical adjustment. 'Dave, let the Beast take the free kicks.'

It almost works. Early on in the second half, a free kick from the Beast goes just over the bar.

Fashion Flaw makes a couple of good saves at his near post, and Bridges have several threatening free kicks and corners. Finally, Glass Back is sent on to get his goal. In one of those bizarre Sunday league situations, the sent-off Tel then becomes an official, replacing Glass Back, who was running the line. This doesn't put a stop to his running commentary, though. 'Come on! Get the bloody second ball! Help Crocky out! Well done, Shaggy . . .' he bawls.

But still it's only 1-0 and a little self-belief returns to the Windy Millers' ten men. They even force a corner and Keith comes charging up the field like a colour-blind Peter Schmeichel. He actually connects with the ball, volleying somewhere between the goal and corner flag. This seems to inspire the eccentric goalkeeper – while the ball is up the other end he proceeds to lean on his goalpost and drink a pint of beer that's been delivered to him from the clubhouse.

There's a few midfield scuffles, a handbags-at-ten-paces confrontation and then, amazingly, in the final minute, the Windy Millers equalise. It's a terrible own goal. Under slight pressure from Glass Back, a Bridges defender supplies a textbook finish to a cross into the penalty area. The Windy Millers are going crazy with relief.

'JESUS H. CHRIST! HALLELUJAH!!!' bawls Keith from his goal. 'I told you I'd score. That's my goal,' says substitute Glass Back, who was a good three or four feet away from the defender. A minute later, the final whistle blows.

'Nets!' bawls Keith before the players have a chance to sneak off without putting them away. He then turns his attention to the opposition, already making their way towards their cars. 'You know when you've been Tangoed, lads!'

'Wanker!' comes the response.

'Fuckin' mardy bastards!' mutters Keith.

Back in the dressing container, Gary Glitter is back on the ghetto blaster as the lads get changed straight into their clothes, the refurbished container not running to showers.

'That was a first for me,' says Tel.

'I've seen you hit people before,' says a team-mate.

'Yeah, but I've never been sent off for it before.'

In the Windmill clubhouse, the lads settle down for a beer or four. Solid clubman David Lane returns muddied but excited from the reserves' game. 'We lost 5-3 but it was a moral victory after the way we've been playing. I was really pleased for them because it's the first time in weeks we've played really well.' This man has Tango blood in his veins.

Glass Back is having no luck in claiming the goal. 'He was only about four thousand yards away from the bloke that put it in,' mocks Keith. As round follows round, the guffawing gets louder. Even Billy, fresh from last night's conquest/fiasco, is in the bar, having forgiven the lads for attempting to sabotage his sexual manoeuvres.

It soon becomes clear that the Windy Millers are an institution in Nuneaton – albeit one for the criminally insane. Keith returns home to collect a folder full of club fanzines and his own poems. Also known as The Gay Poet, over the seasons he's written such epics as 'Cheer Up Fatty Lane' and 'How I Got Into Fat Lane's Pants'.

Profiles of ex-stars Captain Deep and Mister Spoons are produced, along with photo albums of numerous club tours. Fat Lane, Fashion Flaw and an old player called Fat Wallet reminisce about climbing through hotel windows, beds being taken apart and reassembled in corridors and unprintable activities with carrots. There are pictures of the side wearing Dennis the Menace wigs in their old red and black hooped kit and a very suspect tartan kit used by the reserves. There are plenty of snaps of mad supporter Dave the Rave and thankfully only one of the entire side bending over and mooning at the camera. It's less the heart and soul than the arse and hole of football.

The Windy Millers personify the spirit of Sunday football with their mix of booze-fuelled earnest endeavour and outright lunacy. They're the oldest adolescents in town. I have found the epicentre of old laddism in the back of a container on top of a quarry at the famous Mile High Stadium in windswept Nuneaton.

And the Tango men are buying me another pint . . .

5 Nine Men Went to Mow

They're under-strength, over-employed and over there. Football is a simple game and at the end of the day it's supposed to be eleven men against eleven, Barry. But in Sunday football it seldom is.

Perhaps it's just bad karma. Maybe it is inappropriate Feng Shui with incorrectly aligned goalposts facing east when they should be facing west. Or perhaps the astrological signs are all wrong. But whatever the cosmological forces at play, getting eleven men out on to a football pitch at 10.30 am on a Sunday morning is a task seemingly doomed to end in disappointment and farce.

Stephen Hawking might be able to predict the shape of the space-time continuum, but even he would struggle to field a side in the London Relegation League. Einstein discovered that for every action there is an opposite reaction, and the reaction of the Sunday league player to a phone call from the manager is usually to stay in bed to spend more time with his hangover. Club secretaries' BT Friends and Family numbers consist of nothing but frequently phoned Lord Lucan-like players. Nothing goes to plan on those grim, rainy winter mornings when players go missing presumed shopping at Ikea. As W. B. Yeats almost put it: 'The centre forward fails to hold, things fall apart . . .'

Had Bryan Robson accrued the experience of most Sunday league club managers, then Middlesbrough would not have been relegated at the end of the 1996–97 season after having three points deducted for failing to field a side at Blackburn. Faced with a squad of players all claiming they couldn't play at Ewood Park because they had to go shopping with the wife at

MFI as the in-laws were down, Robbo should have done the obvious – recruited that geezer sleeping on Fabrizio Ravanelli's sofa, put on his boots himself, started the game with nine men and prayed that the car with Juninho's two Brazilian mates in it would arrive twenty minutes into the match.

Desperation requires subtle manipulation of the rules. That bloke who slept on the right back's floor becomes a vital component of the manager's game plan. 'Ringers' are usually told that if booked they should give the name of the midfielder who emigrated last season but is still registered and mysteriously plays twenty games a season despite having moved to Australia.

One of the best ringer stories comes from a side who were playing a House of Commons XI a few years ago. The MPs turned up with a familiar-looking ringer, a bald bloke who could play a bit. Then the bemused opposition realised that the bald bloke was in fact Bobby Charlton, coaxed into action by an MP sympathetic to Manchester's Olympic bid.

A typical under-strength scenario is described by Lokomotiv's Brian Benson. 'We were playing Santana, this team from Wandsworth, at Tugmutton Common near Orpington, and we only had nine men. We expected to get slaughtered, but then the opposition didn't turn up. We thought we'd get away with it but then, much to our disappointment, eight of them turned up 25 minutes after kick-off, so we had to go ahead. Believe it or not, this was a top-of-the-table clash, and it was nine men versus eight men. But once it kicked off, both sides were really going for it. Then two more of Santana's men turned up at half-time, so they'd got ten and we'd got nine.

'Anyway, we scored midway through the second half. But then one of our players got injured and had to go off, so we were down to eight men against ten, but hanging on grimly to our one-goal lead. Then one of their players got injured, so in the last ten minutes it's our eight against their nine. If there was one more off then the game would have had to have been abandoned as there's a rule that says you can't play with less than eight men.'

But there was yet another twist to Lokomotiv's bewildering

match. 'Only, then disaster struck,' continues Benson. 'In the last ten minutes yet another of our lads got injured and he could hardly stand up. But I made him play on, and told him to run it off as there was no way we were going to blow these three points. We eventually won 1-0 and when he went to hospital he found he'd got a hairline fracture of the ankle.

'In fact, we were all just about standing at the end. It was a bruising match and we were all shattered in the pub. But in a strange kind of way both sides really enjoyed it. It was one of the strangest games you could ever want to play in, and you were never sure just how many players were on the pitch.'

The Sunday player is not easily deterred from playing, even if his weakened side is clearly in for a roasting. If nothing else, there are the financial implications of not fielding a side, as Keith Lee of White Hart Hyde in Cheshire realises: 'There was one game where half the team didn't turn up, and we were down to seven men. I thought I'm not going to pay a £25 fine for not fielding a side, so I got my boots on and played myself. We played 35 minutes each way and got beaten 18-1, but at least I was in pocket!'

Then there are the sides that start the game with nine men awaiting the customary late arrivals. Never mind the so-called gay gene; the latest scientific research will surely soon prove that there is a lateness gene inherent in Sunday footballers. Two Milldean players once actually managed to make the pitch, albeit having missed the kick-off, after clubbing all night in Manchester and returning on the milk train to London.

A trip to Amsterdam almost grounded the Flying Pig's Stewart Cousins. 'Big Rich, our major supporter, has now moved his company to Amsterdam so I flew out on a Thursday night. I flew back early on the Sunday morning just for the football. But the plane was supposed to get back from Amsterdam at nine but it was delayed until 10.45. Still, I did manage to play the second half.' Now that's dedication for you.

But, even with a full side, players can be called off the pitch to fulfil the most unexpected of commitments. In 1993, Holsworthy in the North Devon Kingsley League lost a player in the most unforeseen of circumstances. Secretary James

Cornish complains, 'In one game we were reduced to ten men not by a sending off but by the call-out of our midfield maestro, who sidelines as a local vet, to attend a calving.' So yet another player goes down with a calf problem.

A side can also be reduced to ten men through having a Diego Prima Donna in goal. Mike Pattenden of Millbank in London recalls an opposition keeper who simply sat down in his goal as he claimed he was getting no support from his defence. 'This lousy cross just went in over him and he was sitting there doing a Neville Southall. His team gave him a bit of shit and he was forced to get up after that.'

Another moral dilemma is what to do if you have twelve players and the opposition has ten. Pattenden has seen the ructions this can cause. 'One lad was so incensed at not playing that, rather than be sub, he ran over to join the opposition's ten men just to spite us. He still plays, but his popularity diminished after that and he was frozen out for a bit.'

But if there's one thing worse than starting a game with nine men, it's listening to the so-called reasons as to why half the side haven't turned up. And the invention of the answerphone has made it even easier for the cowardly player to give his excuses for non-availability to a cassette rather than front it out with the manager.

As any club secretary knows, excuses are one of the few things the players excel in. Many would make fine politicians. They are masters at sophistry, being economic with the truth, economic with the actuality or resorting to blatant lying. If the typical Sunday league player was a US president then he'd be impeached even quicker than Nixon.

Some excuses are ingenious, others just limp. At Perfidious Albion, legendary wet excuses include, 'I've had a hard day at work', 'I was stuck on the Central Line' (even though four other players arrived on it), the pathetic 'I want to go for a walk with my girlfriend on Hampstead Heath', and even, for an evening match thankfully, 'I've been to the pub first.' Ed, the club's secretary, complains, 'I've just got my phone bill and there's about thirty calls all for eight seconds. They just go, "Can you play?" "No." '

Jeff Spencer of Brookmans Park in Hertfordshire finds his players pleading amnesia. 'They always say, "I didn't get a phone call" when I know they did, or they say, "I was told it was 9.30 in the pub", when they know it's always 9 am.'

The winner of an *FC* magazine competition for excuses came from Old Ilfordians who once had a player claim, 'My dog had a heart attack after falling off his skateboard.' Really clever players offer the combined excuse. The harassed Ilford secretary also heard the memorable joint excuse of, 'The wife's got PMT' from the midfield schemer, backed up by, 'His wife's got PMT and thrown away my boots' (midfield schemer's best friend).

The lads of Laindon offered up such feeble tales as, 'My duvet cover came up in the night and I got a draught on my back giving me backache', 'I had to take my library books back', 'I went to Birmingham to see *The Clothes Show* with my girlfriend', and, 'I was at a masons' do in Manchester', while Old Oscott FC produced a memorable pre-emptive strike of 'I didn't turn up this week as I didn't think you'd pick me as I failed to turn up last week.' Colombos FC in Portsmouth managed 'I had to go to a fondue party' and 'I didn't want to sustain a facial injury and ruin my wedding photographs'. Wimps, every one of them.

One of the all-time greats came from the ball player at a London club who pleaded, 'My vasectomy stitches have come undone.' Injury is a common plea, with everything from 'The groin strain's playing up again' to 'I had toothache'.

Then there's the unbelievable scenario excuse like 'I was coming back from a wedding and the car broke down when I hit a sheep eight miles south of Aberdeen' or 'I went to a party and my car got towed away'. Others go for pathos, such as 'My dog died' or 'My girlfriend's just left me and I'm just not in the right frame of mind to perform, boss'.

But the excuse that no one will tolerate, however, is the 'I was having sex' plea. No self-respecting player ever puts sex before football, so if you find yourself in this situation invent a vasectomy problem or dead dog.

Managers and secretaries might be in need of counselling as ever feebler excuses reach them on their answerphones, but they should be consoled a little by the knowledge that there is a rare type of footballer who is actually *too* keen to play.

An incredulous Jeff Spencer of Brookmans Park has one player who is surely the Arnold Schwarzenegger of his league. Even a car smash couldn't stop him playing. 'One of our players, John, drove his BMW into a ditch on the way to a game. He was going to call the AA but decided to do it after the game. He jumped into another player's car that was passing, and played in the match. He played quite well, despite his accident.

'Then he phoned the AA after the game and went back to the accident site. When he got back to his BMW in the ditch, it had stickers all round it and was surrounded by police. They didn't seem impressed with his argument that he had to get to the match on time. He got a fine for leaving it in a dangerous position. He won our Nightmare-of-the-Year award at the end-of-season awards ceremony for his crash. One of the lads works for the *Sun* and he mocked up a front page with a picture of an upside-down BMW and John revealing the truth about his "Death Crash Terror".'

But luckily that kind of dedication is rare. The understrength side will be with us as long as the game survives. And if nothing else, it's good for Telecom shareholders. The use of cellular phones must soar at 10.25 am every Sunday morning as managers seek a one to one with anyone who's got a pair of boots.

6 Who Ate All the Pies?

Sunday league football is the natural habitat of the fat bloke. Every side has at least one, and sometimes you find whole teams of fat blokes rampaging across the fields like those herds of running dinosaurs in *Jurassic Park*.

The corpulent star might hate the thought of attending a gym, but Sunday football at least gives him the illusion of sporting activity. He believes that a beer gut is a positive aid in cushioning the ball and that an extra ring of flab (sorry, 'muscle') around the waist provides him with a low centre of gravity, ideal for slipping defenders in the penalty area. After all, you never lose your skill, even if you do look like Jabba the Hut and are about as mobile as one of those two-storey high giant trucks used in South American open-cast copper mines.

Each week, brightly coloured nylon is stretched over ever-burgeoning girths. And, as summer changes to autumn, the kit gets smaller from too many hot washes and strains to cover the lad's growing guts. Like the universe, the footballer's stomach started from something infinitesimal and is now seemingly expanding outward and onward for billions of years, until presumably all matter will implode beneath the weight of one gigantic gut that originated on Hackney Marshes.

No wonder Danny Baker is so into Sunday football – he looks like most of the players. A caller to Baker's radio show once recounted the tale of how a Sunday league goalkeeper gathered a cross and called one of his midfield players towards him. He appeared to be having an animated tactical discussion but was in fact stuffing the ball up the midfielder's jumper. The player then ran as fast as he could towards the opposition goal line, dodged the keeper, pulled up his shirt and deposited the ball like an egg in the back of the net. The goal was given.

'For the life of me I can't think why it shouldn't have been given and why we don't see this tactic attempted at least once every game,' mused Baker, perhaps sensing this was the only way Millwall might achieve success. The tale of the ball up the jumper routine might well be apocryphal, but the point is that in most Sunday league games you wouldn't notice a bloke with a football stuffed up his shirt.

Of all positions, it's goalkeeper that most attracts the fat bloke. Neville Southall and Kevin Pressman are natural Sunday league custodians.

When the Wheatsheaf from St Helen's, Bishop Auckland, were having a dismal run in the 1994–95 season, they decided to do what any desperate side would – draft in a 21-stone goalkeeper. You can't see Glenn Hoddle employing quite the same tactics and promoting Buster Bloodvessel to the England side, but it does have a kind of relentless logic to it. After all, they do say that goalkeepers should make themselves look big.

Pub regular John Carter was the man entrusted with blocking the bulk of the opposition chances. Sadly, the giant keeper let in a further 158 goals that season, including the Wheatsheaf's heaviest defeat, a 20-1 drubbing from rivals Crook Athletic. The podgy custodian made national headlines as the Wheatsheaf finished with an incredible minus one point, having drawn one game but having two points deducted for failing to field a team for one match. The team's sad record read: played 30, won 0, drawn 1, lost 29, for 37, against 208, points −1.

Carter, then 31, had been recovering from the ordeal in his local pub, the Locomotive, where he discussed his predicament over a lunchtime pint. Had his manager ever insisted he lose weight?

'I wouldn't go on a diet. I like my grub too much,' he said, a man of principle who trains on his favourite foods of kebabs and Chinese takeaways. Although John enjoyed a few healing pints after each defeat, he felt that some of his team-mates might have overdone it the previous evening. 'I think some of them were still drunk when they played,' remarked the rueful shot stopper. It wasn't all John's fault, though: 'I pulled off some close-range saves that I was quite proud of.'

John had played three years previously when he was 'a bit lighter', but doesn't recommend a playing weight of 21 stone as 'there's too much pressure on the knees and ankles'. Sadly for the Wheatsheaf, the tubby star has now hung up his boots as he feels he's 'too heavy'. And there are the injuries too: 'My back's killing me from picking the ball out of the net.'

However, John Carter and all other fat Sunday league keepers can take comfort from history, as they could yet receive an offer from Chelsea. Keith Farnsworth's *Sheffield Football: A History* (Hallamshire Press) contains the tale of William Foulkes, the heaviest League player on record, known throughout the land as 'Fatty Foulkes' or 'Little Willie'.

Fatty Foulkes joined Sheffield United in 1894 weighing thirteen stone, but when he moved to Chelsea in 1905 he had ballooned to 23 stone. Back then they had proper players at top clubs with no worries about absurd notions of diet and fitness. Foulkes was a Sunday leaguer in spirit and once ate all fifteen breakfasts laid out for his United team-mates before the 1899 FA Cup semi-final. Later in his career at Chelsea, Foulkes arrived at a northern station to find men with sandwich boards reading: 'Come and see the 24-and-a-half-stone goalkeeper.' 'I'll give 'em 24 stun!' cried the bulky custodian before charging at the men, forcing them to drop their sandwich boards and run.

An all-round character, Foulkes was surprisingly agile for a big man, particularly when chasing match officials. After conceding a goal he felt was offside in the 1902 FA Cup Final, a *naked* Foulkes pursued the referee after the game.

Linesman J. T. Howcroft recalled: 'He was in his birthday suit outside the dressing rooms and I saw F. J. Wall, secretary of the FA, plead with him to rejoin his colleagues. But Bill was out for blood and I shouted to the referee to lock his cubicle door. But what a sight! The thing I'll never forget is Foulkes, so tremendous in size, striding along the corridor without a stitch of clothing.'

Among more recent professionals, the rotund performer has

always attracted attention from the fans. 'He's fat, he's round, he bounces off the ground! Sammy Lee!' was the chant opposition fans used to taunt Liverpool's solid midfielder with. Life is not easy for the footballer with the fuller figure. At Coventry, Mickey Quinn (the fastest player in the Premiership over one yard) had to endure cries of 'Sumo!' and 'Are you Blobby in disguise?' Paul Gascoigne was pelted with Mars Bars at Newcastle, and, when he was injured at Spurs, their fans were teased with cries of, 'Where's your fat boy gone?' Even Scunthorpe once boasted a beefy reserve in the form of Ian Botham.

Jan Molby is another Liverpool midfielder known for his girth, and after a series of motoring misdemeanours, there were terrace chants of, 'He's fat, he's round, his car is in the pound!' And when Tomas Brolin claimed he'd got his hunger back playing for Crystal Palace, it looked as if he'd satisfied it at the pizza parlours of Streatham.

But the podgy pro is getting rarer. 'The big backsides have gone,' says Don Howe, the FA's technical co-ordinator. 'Today, players know more about the right high-carbohydrate diet, whereas, when I was playing, England lost 5-3 to Hungary and everyone said it was because they ate steaks and we should do the same.'

Luckily, very little of that let-them-eat-steak nonsense, or indeed the modern sporting fad of pasta, has permeated through to the Sunday leagues. Even if the professionals are eating wisely, many weekend sides are like Dickens' Thomas Gradgrind: they stick to fats, fats, fats, nothing but fats. To spot the podgier players, just observe who races to the kit bag first and grabs the baggiest shorts.

Denis Wilson of Harold Wood Hospital FC in Essex has moved from centre forward to defence to goalkeeper as both the years and his girth have advanced. 'Unfortunately, I have to play in a pink shirt, so you get all the obvious cries of "Mr Blobby!"' he says. 'The lads also call me "The Tin Man" because they say I can't bend over. However, I don't need a padded shirt and thanks to my weight it doesn't hurt so much when I go down now.'

Wilson's funniest moment was when his fellow fattie centre

half played in goal in a friendly. 'Their centre forward lobbed the ball in, and immediately turned round and cried, "I've lobbed the Blob!" All our side were falling about laughing. He's always called the Blob now, and we were going to get some special "I've lobbed the Blob" T-shirts printed for our awards ceremony, but we thought he might be too upset.'

Inevitably, fat players receive nicknames from their teammates. The Windy Millers in Nuneaton refer to two of their side as 'FB1' and 'FB2', the acronyms standing for 'Fat Bastard 1' and 'Fat Bastard 2'. The side has also had a player named 'Dumpertruck' after a Sumo wrestler, a 'Statto' said to bear a resemblance to *Fantasy Football*'s portly and pyjama-clad statistician, and a 'Barney Rubble' named after the *Flintstones* character.

David Lane (FB1) recalls how he earned his nickname. 'This lad from London came up and shouted 'You fat bastard!' from the touchline. The ref thought it was one of the opposition players and gave us a free kick, so the name stuck.'

Martin Bester of the Masons Arms in Yeovil has a weighty player in his side called 'The Lummox' – 'It's a Somerset word meaning a big lumbering carthorse.'

Some lummoxes can be shamed into losing weight. Wirral side the Ship Inn had a sweepstake on how much a portly player weighed at their awards ceremony. 'He was placed on the scales, which revealed he was fifteen stone, more than even his wife suspected, and that public humiliation shamed him into losing a lot of weight. He's now moved on to a very good side,' says secretary Darren Murphy.

Other sides point to the advantages of fat players: it takes an age to go round them; their tackles usually take both man and ball into the stratosphere; and, with all that weight behind them, when they do connect with the ball properly, a fat bloke's shot can knock a non-fat goalkeeper through the back of the net. And if they're like 'Fat Tim' of the aptly named Three Tuns in Hull, they can prove a secret weapon.

'We'd had a terrible start to the season, losing four games and not scoring,' recalls Derek Russell. 'Fat Tim was a sub, desperate to get on, and we were losing 3-0. Then with his first touch he hit a twenty-yard screamer into the top corner. He went bounding down the field like a fairy elephant because he'd scored our first goal of the season!'

As they say in football, it's never over until the fat lady sings – or the fat keeper collapses. Andy Taylor of the New Inn Sidley recalls the day his sixteen-stone goalie's hamstring went. 'We didn't even know Coley the Goalie had a hamstring beneath all that flesh. It took eight of us to lift him up and then he was only about four inches off the ground. The ref was killing himself laughing.'

But if you're a fat player who receives stick from the opposition, then it might pay to examine your taunters' waistlines, says comedian Phill 'Porky' Jupitus, star of *Never Mind the Buzzcocks* and a man who enjoys a fuller figure himself. He is regularly greeted on stage at stand-up comedy gigs with chants of 'Who ate all the pies?' Phill is a West Ham fan and a former cartoonist for the award-winning fanzine *Fortune's Always Hiding*, where he drew under the name of Porky.

'I went to West Ham once and there was this bloke shouting, 'Molby, you fat bastard!' and I looked at this fan and he was massive, wearing a skin-tight shellsuit and all nineteen of his chins were still wobbling!' recalls Phill.

Indeed, let him who is without a beer gut throw the first fattist insult. But before you put your side on a diet, Jupitus believes a high quotient of fatsos in your side could be good for business. 'If you've got all these fat blokes rippling their flesh in nylon football shirts, imagine the static electricity generated. If you could harness it and sell it to National Power, you could boost your transfer funds no end. Fat blokes could be an alternative source of power!' So that's what they mean by a midfield dynamo.

The fat player will be with us for as long as Sunday football. Many sides now have crates of isotonic sports drinks on the touchline for half-time refreshment. The coach has oranges at half-time and water for rehydration after the game. And it makes no difference at all. On the pitch are a set of fat bastards. Sports nutrition – you've a fat chance, mate.

7 'On Me 'Ead, Pervy!'

'And Nobby Rash is through. He goes round Pervy and Captain Deep. He's just got Eggs And Bacon to beat. The keeper's palmed it away at the second attempt, and, oh, I say, Trevor, Chinola has trapped it on the line, dribbled it out of defence and set up Chicken with a perfect through ball!'

John Motson might be able to name the South Korean sweeper without hesitation, but even the redoubtable Motto would have trouble keeping up with the ever-expanding nomenclature of parks football. Nothing reflects the blokeish camaraderie of our national sport better than a team's choice of nicknames. Count Dracula, Sharky, Yogga, Chinola, Bubble, Chicken, The Beast, Amos Leisure, Pervy, Tallish Paul, Taz, Jugsy, Captain Deep, Nobby Rash, Stevie Blunder, Eggs And Bacon and countless other lads with ludicrous monikers can all be found performing on the playing fields of England.

There's nothing as prosaic as Incey, Becks, Keaney or Gazza in the Sunday leagues; here creativity and wit combine to create a veritable thesaurus-worth of strange monikers. Of course, nicknames at this level are not always PC. At one club in the London Relegation League, a midfielder called Dave turned up with a couple of 'ringers' to complete the side. Throughout the game they kept calling him 'Hog'. At the end of the game, the whole team were baffled, and asked Dave's mates why they called him Hog. 'Because he slept with a pig last night!' came the memorable reply. Germaine Greer would not have been amused.

If a player has a suspect taste in women then his team-mates quickly notice. 'My all-time favourite was a player called

Sledge, because he was always getting pulled by dogs,' says Neil Treadwell of Westlea Wanderers in Leamington Spa. 'I'm nicknamed either The Curry Monster or Billy The Fish as I eat and drink a fair bit. We also had Three Ball, which was something to do with the wedding tackle area, Cracker, who liked to damage players' shin pads, and Peanut, so named because of his eating habits. Our current side includes Rug Rat, who looks like the cartoon character, and Flip-Flop Head, which is to do with the way he drinks.'

David Lane of the Windy Millers remembers that the club once had two aesthetically challenged players. 'We started off calling this lad Gargoyle and then it changed to Ugly. Then his mate turned up who was even uglier. So we called them Ugly and Even Uglier.' Iain Dowie must be relieved that he's never, as yet, had to perform for the Windy Millers.

Another corpulent Windy Millers star rejoices in the twin nicknames of Mel Smith and The Beast. 'He's not very keen on being called The Beast,' admits secretary Paul Kettell, 'but he's five foot ten and built like Jan Molby.' Then there's Static, Amos Leisure, Fashion Flaw, Captain Deep, The Scab and Twinkle Toes.

'We presented Twinkle Toes with a ballet slipper at our awards ceremony. He was a very delicate player and wouldn't go for 50/50 balls,' explains Kettell. 'There's a big rivalry between Bedworth and Nuneaton. They call us treacle towners as they say that when we're hit we stay stuck to the floor. The Scab comes from Bedworth and plays in Nuneaton which is how he got his name. Static is a big 40-year-old guy who plays up front and doesn't move around much. What our keeper Keith 'Fashion Flaw' Jones wears wouldn't look good even if it was in fashion. He looks just like Noddy Holder.'

Then there was the intense brooding figure of Captain Deep, the Mr Darcy of Nuneaton. 'Captain Deep, who's now departed, was a really good player but very deep thinking. He couldn't understand us and we couldn't understand him,' continues David Lane. 'Amos Leisure was really called Mark Wilson. We nicknamed him Amos because he wore terrible tank tops like Amos Brierley in *Emmerdale Farm*. His leisurewear was so bad that it then became Amos Leisure. We had one awards ceremony where everyone had to wear tank tops in his honour.'

At the Sun in Reading it seems no one has a real name. The team is managed by Dude ('a cool Fonz-like character') who can pick from a squad including Dick Seaman in goal ('his real name Richard combined with Arsenal's keeper'), plus Madge ('he's magic on the field'), Fat Larry ('we saw this character in an ice-cream advert called Fat Larry who looked just like him'), Oily ('a slimy sod'), Bart ('he looks like Bart Simpson'), Wayne ('a 40-year-old with a ponytail who looks like Wayne from *Wayne's World*'), Mad Dog ('he wouldn't say boo to a goose but he once broke a player's leg'), Eddie Munster ('he's got a very high forehead'), Ray Reardon ('spitting image of the snooker star') and Count Dracula ('he looks like Bela Lugosi and is scared of crosses'). And there's even Taff to run the line and ace reporter Allan Shaftbottom to write the club newsletter.

Goalkeepers inevitably suffer from their team-mates' wit. Colinthians in Birmingham once played with a man called Flapper as custodian. South London side Milldean used to play with Stevie Mandry aka Stevie Blunder between the sticks. After a heavy defeat, one of the Milldean players declared in the showers, 'We'd have been better off playing with Stevie Wonder in goal!' A team-mate replied, 'Stevie Blunder more like!' and the unfortunate nickname stuck. In fact, he was so good at blundering that he's now become the club's manager.

A defender's performance can have long-lasting results. Blueline Harlech in Liverpool have an unfortunate centre half called 'Roundabout', so named because everybody goes round him. Such is the preponderance of nicknames that a player at the Merseyside club Poulton Victoria, winners of the 1996-97 Carlsberg Cup, even has the nickname Simon 'No Nickname' Lewis.

The Flying Pig in Cambridge are another club with a nickname for every player – they even have them for their fans. They used to have Clint 'Comedy Gloves' Burberry in goal, who was replaced by Stewart 'Best Bloke' Cousins (winner of the Carlsberg Best Bloke in Football Award in 1996) who also goes under the moniker of 'Abo', short for Aborigine, as he tends to go walkabout up to the halfway line while in goal. Cousins possesses so many personalities that he must be on police files as a potential serial killer; he's also the official 'Club Tall Person'. The previous Club Tall Person was Paul Keeble, who upon the arrival of the 6 ft 4 ins Cousins was demoted to 'Tallish Paul'.

A player's occupation can be an absolute gift to the dressing-room wags: in real life the Pig's Adam Galbraith is a ballet dancer at a school in London. He's now known as 'Madam' and was presented with a tutu at the club's alternative awards ceremony, which he wore throughout the team curry.

Then there's Simon 'Nosty' Rivers, who has Nostradamus-like long hair and a beard and made a couple of freak predictions about results which came true; Gerry 'My Little Pony' Gibson who has a long ponytail which he's very proud of; Ian 'Zico' Read who's the oldest player and refuses to head the ball; and Jimmy 'Seventies Man' Cameron, who wears very wide flares and platform shoes. The Adams family, Jonny and Chris, are big lads known as 'Rhino' and 'Lumpy'. Peter Hindley earned the inevitable nickname of 'Myra', while the player-manager whose real name is Michael Jackson is known as 'Wacko'. The rest of the side look forward to Jackson being booked for being Bad, as referees always refuse to believe that he's really called Michael Jackson.

And as for the Flying Pig fans, the club boasts Captain Cooker (he wears a pig hat to every game and Captain Cooker is a New Zealand pig), Pacer (a fan who restlessly paces the touchline), Killer (a woman called Tracey who plays a mean game of darts) and Peter 'Dodgy Old Geezer' Cousins (at his first match he stood away from the other supporters and one of them asked, 'Who's that dodgy old geezer?'). The club secretary Joanne 'Mrs Belly' Griffiths (so named during her pregnancy) lives with Stewart 'Best Bloke' Cousins. Their baby son Jack was called 'Piglet' in honour of his role as the Flying Pig's youngest supporter.

Richard Macdonald of Saracens in Coventry remembers one legendary keeper. 'He was called Eggs And Bacon because he made a meal of everything. Our players would shout it out every time he made a save or dive. He emigrated to Australia eventually.' Mick Pearce of south London side Good For The Game In General will never forget a keeper called Taz, named after the cartoon character based on a Tasmanian Devil. (Julian Dicks was so impressed with the loveable devil that he had a tattoo of him.) 'He had a satanic stare and a wide-open mouth, and used to explode all the time. He made Peter Schmeichel look like a mouse. No one dared tell him about his nickname.'

Other Good For The Game In General nicknames include the Plankton Brothers ('they're quite intelligent but together they get really crude and do ridiculous things') and Trevor 'Pervy' Pommills ('he'd look at anything in a skirt, and was even smutty and rude while playing'). The side even has its own virtual reality star. 'Once an opposition player shouted, "Mark Super Mario!" ' remembers Pearce. 'We looked at Lloyd's moustache and realised that even though he's black he was the spit of Super Mario, so the name stuck.'

Many players are likened to animals. At Milldean they had a character called Sharky, because he's said to look like a shark and his tackles result in one-legged wingers. Chicken plays on right wing for the New Inn Sidley in Bexhill, East Sussex. 'He's not got much of a brain and runs around like a headless chicken,' explains secretary Andy Taylor. 'We've called him that for ten years, although he hasn't developed a goal-scoring clucking celebration yet. His real name is Darren, but even his wife calls him Chicken. He's in the catering corps of the army which is rather apt.' And just to complete the image, Chicken's favourite drink is a lethal real ale called Old Speckled Hen.

The West Coast Armadillos had a player called Peugeot because he claimed to have had 306 lovers, along with Bungalow who had nothing upstairs. At the Masons Arms in Yeovil they have Mousse, so christened because of the amount of mousse he puts in his hair, and Fishy, whose real surname is Herring. Other New Inn Sidley stars include Chinola – 'He's a big tall centre half with about six chins who fancies himself as a dribbler.' Then there was a former player called Bubble. 'He fancied himself as a drinker,' says Taylor, 'but at the end of our drinking games he'd be pushing lager back into his glass as he finished his pint and you'd see bubbles in his lager.'

Mind you, some clubs have noted a decline in the standard of nomenclature. 'When we started in 1982 there was a nickname for everyone, but these days it's just things like Clarky,' sighs Jeff Spencer of Hertfordshire side Brookmans Park. 'We had Errol who was named after Errol Flynn because he had a big whatsit. I was called Headcase as I play in goal. There was a guy called Chairman. His real name was Nicky May, but the paper printed it as Mayo. So we called him Chairman Mayo and then Chairman. And there's a bloke who's still called Jugsy fifteen years on. He used to score lots of hat-tricks for which he got a jug of beer. And we had Robin Nash who we called Nobby Rash and a guy who was a punk and had a Luftwaffe jacket, who we called Luft. I met a guy the other day who remembered playing us fifteen years ago. When his team came off the pitch they couldn't stop laughing after hearing us all calling "Chairman!" and "Jugsy!" '

Mind you, too many nicknames can cause nightmares for a club secretary. 'When I saw their real names written down on the subs list I couldn't work out who anyone was,' says Phil Colver of Colinthians. 'On the pitch we had lads like Digger, Mezza, Brick, Tufty, Humpy, Flapper and Smiler. Some of the nicknames were really obscure. There was a bald player called Leigh whom everyone called Yogga. This was because when he was younger he had a lot of hair and Yogga had derived from Yogi Bear.'

Mind you, some players' real names are more surreal than even the most bizarre of nicknames. 'We've got a Bosnian player called Elvis Music,' says Colver. 'Thank goodness he's never been booked, because I'm sure the ref would send him off for taking the mickey!'

THE NICKNAME XI

Eggs And Bacon

Chicken

Captain Deep

Count Dracula

The Beast

Fat Bastard 1

Pervy

Chinola

Chairman

Yogga

Nobby Rash

Subs:

Brick

Tufty

Sharky

8 A Bunch of Animals

Sadly the Sunday game is beset by the problem of pitch invasions. No, these are not rampaging fans throwing seats, or supporters demanding the sacking of the board and attempting to storm the executive suite (aka the saloon bar). The invaders are a different species of fan entirely, and include dogs, horses, cows, rabbits and moles.

Take the example of the tense 1997 local derby between rival pub teams Portland Arms (now Hollyhill FC) and the Coach and Horses in Gateshead. The score was 4-4 and the game seemingly deadlocked as the final whistle approached. Suddenly Portland brought on the most unusual of supersubs with two fresh pairs of legs – Nipper, a seven-month-old bull terrier owned by Portland skipper Steve Wraith.

They think it's all Rover . . . It is now! Brilliantly slipping his defensive leash and ignoring the fact that no Portland player had gone off, Nipper ran on to the pitch and robbed the Coach and Horses centre half with a dogged tackle. Without paws for thought, he evaded the Coach and Horses full back and rode two further challenges before slipping the ball to Portland striker Gary Roberts, who gleefully whacked the ball into the net. Clearly feeling that this was a piece of wuff justice, the referee allowed the goal and blew the final whistle seconds later, leaving him in the doghouse with the irate Coach and Horses players.

Owner Steve Wraith refused to say if contract negotiations had been opened with the terrier-like midfielder, but did admit: 'It was our most dramatic win of the season. And Nipper was the difference between the two teams.'

Nor was this the first time a dog had intervened in a crucial

Sunday league match. The *Virgin Book of Football Records* reveals that, in the 1985 Staffordshire Sunday Cup, a dog scored a goal for the Knave of Clubs against Newcastle Town. 'The number canine', as Brian Clough might have referred to him, intercepted a shot that was going wide and bundled it over the line.

Technically, both these goals should have been disallowed. 'The minute the dog comes on it's an outside agent and the referee has to give a drop ball,' says Peter Willis of the Referees' Association. Dogs can be more successful in stopping goals, however. 'If a dog makes contact with the ball and prevents a certain goal then the referee can't award a goal. He must stop the game and restart with a drop ball,' adds Willis.

It was significant that, when Nike filmed its famous advert featuring the likes of Eric Cantona, Robbie Fowler, David Seaman and Ian Wright playing on Hackney Marshes, the end of the game was marked by numerous dogs invading the pitch from the touchline. The bloke walking his dog and taking in the game has long been the symbol of Sunday league football – and he can even be collared into playing by a side with only nine men. When Phil Colver of Birmingham side Colinthians was playing for his old club Dynamo Brandhall, he recalls: 'This lad used to watch us every week with his dog. Eventually, someone asked him if he played, and he turned out to be a really good player.'

At least the well-behaved canine spectator does sometimes receive appreciation from the players. The wags at the Three Tuns in Hull have two supporters – the inevitable man and his dog. 'At our awards ceremony we presented him with a trophy as supporter of the year and gave the dog a tin of doggie chunks,' says Derek Russell. Presumably the Three Tuns then went on to Winalot.

Dogs have had quite an influence on the professional game too. West Ham's Julian Dicks is so keen on keeping bull terriers that he has built kennels behind his house and plans to breed them when he retires. The most famous footballing dog of all time was Pickles, the collie who discovered the stolen Jules Rimet World Cup trophy in his front garden in Norwood,

London, in March 1966. He became a national hero, before tragically being strangled by his lead while chasing a cat in the same year.

In 1970, Brentford goalkeeper Chic Brodie's career was ended by a rogue canine. He was stretchered off after colliding with a dog that had run on to the pitch, and his knee injury was so bad that he never played again. And, at the end of the 1986–87 season, a police dog called Ginger saved Torquay's League status – by biting Torquay defender Jim McNichol during a game with Crewe. Torquay were 2-1 down and the game was stopped while McNichol received treatment. During the injury time added on for McNichol's injury, Torquay's Paul Dobson equalised and tail-enders Lincoln lost their place in the League instead of Torquay.

Many Sunday players arrive with their dogs in tow. Martin Carne, a former star of Cornish side St Columb Major, remembers a farmer called Richard who would turn up in a battered Nissan pick-up truck. 'He was a big bruiser of a centre half and he'd arrive with hay bales and electric fencing in the back of the truck and his two sheepdogs in the front. I think they probably helped to intimidate the opposition as they'd bite their heads off given half a chance.'

Sometimes the dog doesn't even have to be there to intimidate the opposition. Nick 'The Cat' Royle recalls his time playing for *Time Out* magazine in the London Relegation League, when his team-mate Nigel would turn up in a dog van. 'It was a tiny mini-van, and the back was filthy and sealed off with wire mesh. Nigel would have about five players squashed into the dog section and when they all came bounding out the opposition must have thought they'd taken on a team of rabid animals. This psychological ploy worked for the first five minutes, but unfortunately the opposition then realised we were crap.'

Players' dogs have also been known to disrupt training sessions. 'One of our lads had one of those English "Winston Churchill" bulldogs called Seth and he took it to a training session,' recalls John Collings of Durham side Murton Village Inn. 'Seth took the ball and no one could get it off him. The dog just stood over the ball and nobody could get near it. Then he took Seth to watch him and it disrupted the game. The referee warned him and then told him to remove the dog, as it was getting so excited players were wary of getting near it. The lad who owned it was called Gary Armstrong, so the dog must have been Seth Armstrong, which gave us all a laugh.' Other dogs have intimidated whole teams: 'Once there was this pit bull terrier locked in the changing room,' recalls George Ward of Milldean. 'We were waiting to get changed but no one could get in. All 22 of us were left cowering outside until the owner turned up.'

Of course, if your team doesn't have a dog as mascot, you can always use a player instead. Mick Pearce of London side Good For The Game In General reveals: 'We have a player called Simon who we say is the dog of the team. On the pitch he runs round chasing his own tail and we always ask him if he has sex doggie style. When he withdrew from the club tour we said he was the missing dog mascot and in the tour programme we stuck his head on a picture of a dog.'

Any pitch on a public park has the inevitable problem of dog mess. This is the curse of every linesman. 'When I'm running the line and we kick off I'm often still busy finding a couple of sticks to carry the dog turds,' says Martin Bester of the Masons Arms in Yeovil.

Ian Morgan, the ex-QPR player who is now park manager at Hackney Marshes as well as West Ham's community officer, says that Cantona and Co. had no problem with dog mess on their visit. 'There's been a by-law since January that you can't foul parks and we have loads of dog bins to help the owners. I was walking across the pitches the other day with Orient manager Tommy Taylor and we saw a man with three dogs cleaning up their mess in a plastic bag, so it must be having an effect.'

But, dog mess aside, the average mutt is keen to help his two-legged friends. Peter Willis has even encountered a canine linesman: 'At Crook Town in the Northern League there was a sheepdog that used to run up and down the line behind the linesman for the whole game. The minute that flag went up the dog stopped dead still. I used to watch the dog as much as the game. It never interfered with the game, and I'm sure that dog judged offside better than the linesman!'

But, ultimately, it's for running on the pitch that man's best friend will be remembered in the Sunday leagues. Phil Colver of Colinthians claims that a labrador knocked his side out of the Holder Cup a couple of years ago: 'We were playing in a cup tie at Sutton Coldfield and this lad went on a run. It looked a certain goal and he was about to shoot when this labrador ran on and got in his way. The dog just wanted to be part of what was going on, but it stood right in front of him and effectively closed him down, better than some defenders I've seen. The rest of us just stood there open-mouthed. That dog cost us a place in the Holder Cup.'

Of course, it's not just dogs that can hamper the progress of the Sunday league stalwart. More animals than made it into Noah's Ark seem to have invaded the parks of the land.

Bovine pitch invasions have resulted in the New Inn Sidley having to never mind the bullocks. Andy Taylor recalls: 'We used to play some yokels at Staplecross and cattle came on the pitch. We had to get 'em off the pitch in the mornings. During one game the cows came on again at half-time as someone had left the gate open and we all had to herd them off.'

Cows can even be a problem in London. Referee Janet Walmsley recalls cows on the pitch at Wanstead Flats. 'Everyone had to get involved and we had two teams shooing these cows off the pitch. The worst thing was the big cow-pats they left behind . . .' Clearly not a pitch suitable for sliding tackles.

Stafford Sunday League side GEC Woolpack suffered from disappearing goal nets, going through three pairs in two seasons. 'At first we thought the fibre in the nets had gone rotten and asked the manufacturers for replacements,' said secretary Derek Burt. 'The problem was solved when the groundsman spotted a group of rabbits hidden in the long grass behind the goal line.' The club has now moved to a rabbit-free ground.

Phil Colver of Colinthians reports a plague of rabbits from

the nearby BR land on his team's pitch breeding quicker than footballers, while the Windy Millers in Nuneaton have had similar problems. 'We had a meeting with the committee about rabbits on the pitch. I said, "We've installed these rabbit toilets but we can't get the bleeders to sit on them." It took them a few minutes to get what I was going on about,' says the man with a lot of rabbit, secretary David Lane.

In Chichester, rabbit invasions became so numerous in 1997 that the *Chichester Observer* wrote: 'Teams frequently have to reconstruct part of the pitch with a bag of soil before a ball is kicked.' The most drastic of solutions was employed. Harold Godfrey, chairman of the playing fields committee, announced: 'We can't allow shooting because it is a place where members of the public go, so we are back to ferreters.' Imagine one of those down your Nike shorts.

And sometimes there are even more carthorses than usual on the pitch. John Collings of Murton Village Inn in Durham has suffered equine pitch invasions: 'We used to play one team where they had to clear horses off the pitch before every game.'

Even moles – presumably blinder than most refs but able to play in the hole – have presented a problem for the Masons Arms. Martin Bester recalls: 'We played a friendly one night and we kicked the molehills down at the start, but as the game progressed more of them appeared. The moles were still active despite 22 blokes running around on top of them.'

But even interventions from live dogs, rabbits, moles, cows and horses seem positively prosaic compared to the player who was felled by a frozen fish in Dewsbury, West Yorkshire. When the Bull's Head striker Damien McManus scored an injury-time winner against the Railway, his team-mates tried to get the monkfish to kiss him during the post-match drink. They emerged from the gents brandishing the fish, but in the kissing mêlée McManus suffered a cut nose and face after encountering the monster from the deep. In a sporting injury that was even more bizarre than a celebratory Tony Adams dropping Steve Morrow and breaking his arm, eighteen-year-old Damien collapsed with blood gushing from his nose and was rushed to hospital. And to think it's usually the fish that gets battered.

The fishy tale was somewhat embellished for the tabloids, which claimed incorrectly that Damien had grabbed the club's mascot, a three-and-a-half stone frozen monkfish, and careered round the pitch holding it above his head.

'We bought the monkfish at a fishmonger in Dewsbury as it was the ugliest thing we'd ever seen,' explained McManus, a self-employed plumber and heating engineer, who has no ambition to be a deep-frying centre forward. The fish was thought to resemble a member of the side, who wishes to retain anonymity, although his initials are AW. 'It's a horrible thing, like a bucket with teeth,' adds Bull's Head landlord Tim Wood. 'But we liked to run around intimidating the opposition with it.'

Since that fishy excursion, the Black Bull have taken the frozen fish to every game, home and away, in a special freezer bag, although it's not as yet worth a plaice in the side.

'The nurses all burst out laughing and the lads ribbed me something rotten, but I suppose it's a bit of soccer history. I can't imagine anyone else has been put in hospital by a frozen monkfish,' said McManus, who must have been grateful he wasn't left nursing a tense nervous haddock.

Which just goes to show: you should never work with children, animals, footballers or frozen fish. But that wasn't the end of the story. The monkfish, who was now something of a local celebrity, was kidnapped two days after the bizarre injury. But it wasn't long before the slippery one bit back.

'The last time the lads say they saw it was on a table outside a pub,' claims Tim Wood. 'Eventually it turned up under the seat in a nearby restaurant and it was rotting away. The restaurant had to get in Rentokil. They don't know how it got there, although some of our lads have been known to eat there, so I have my suspicions. But it was so decomposed that it's now gone to the great fishpond in the sky. You could say we're floundering without it.'

But that hasn't put the side off obtaining a further mascot. 'It's been mentioned that we should purchase a small Vietnamese pot-bellied pig – alive this time,' chuckles Smith. Any player who kisses that surely deserves all he gets.

9 The Gaffer Tapes

Imagine Nigel from *EastEnders* and you have an accurate image of the Sunday league manager. No, make that Nigel on drugs having slept rough in a doorway for six months while living on nothing but Special Brew and chips.

You might have thought Graham Taylor was slightly doolally as he shouted, 'Go on, Platty!', 'Do I not like that!' and 'Carlton . . . Carlton!!!!' On the touchline in Rotterdam, the ex-England boss paced around like a latter-day Captain Ahab, raging at the cosmos and in particular a demonic figure in black who had metaphorically bitten off his leg during the World Cup qualifier against Holland. Yet Taylor is a sane and phlegmatic man compared to most Sunday league managers.

It takes a strange breed to become a Sunday manager. With none of the financial rewards of Alex Ferguson or Kenny Dalglish, he has to stand on freezing touchlines wondering if his players will all turn up, frantically ringing round the squad on his mobile as kick-off approaches and praying that the striker's hangover isn't too bad.

Managers are by nature eccentric and suffer from a form of fashion dyslexia. It's almost as if they want their charges to take the piss out of them. And perhaps they do – Brian Clough used to insist that relaxing the players was the key to successful management, and perhaps a complete lack of sartorial knowledge accompanied by the grooming sense of a muddy sheep is just another tool in the manager's motivational kit.

The manager comes in several recognisable sub-species. A typical example paces the muddy touchline with a beer gut flopping over half-mast jeans, wearing a battered suede jacket and trainers, sporting non-designer stubble and a Kevin Keegan perm, constantly smoking and cursing his hangover as he cries, 'Short balls to feet!'

Most bosses have the dress sense of Worzel Gummidge. Philip Bird of Nottingham side the Duke of Wellington recalls a legendary manager called Gilbert: 'He was a morris dancer and he once appeared on the front of *Country Life*. He'd always turn up wearing a Doctor Who scarf and a World War One trenchcoat and he had long curly hair down to his shoulders. Every week his team talk would be, "Whatever you do, do it with a smile on your face."'

'Remember the three Cs!'

Other managers tend to switch costumes as often as tactics. In York, Mark Pearson of Yorkshire Terriers, formerly known as Cygnet, recalls a legendary boss: 'Our boss Stuart Fairclough turned up on the muddy touchline in his best shoes and wearing a suit, like he thought he was the Leeds manager. Although when the ground was rock hard he turned up in wellies and a horrible green Barbour jacket. Or sometimes he'd totally throw us by wearing the oldest pair of trousers imaginable.' Like most bosses, Fairclough has a catchphrase. 'He shouted "Remember the three Cs!" throughout the game, by which he meant commitment and . . . I can't remember the other two,' confesses Pearson.

Even though most managers make Bob Geldof seem elegant, there are few actual cross-dressers. But Andy Copeland of the Alma Tavern in Middlesex is the sort of gaffer who will go to any lengths to inspire his team, even if it involves wearing women's underwear. 'Whenever we have a big game, he puts ladies' underwear on beneath his clothing,' explains the Tavern's Andrew Nicholls. 'It's normal for Andy, really – he's always trying to think up something to get us going. It's just supposed to be in front of us in the dressing room, but once we threw him outside and he was left standing there in his bra, knickers, stockings and suspenders in front of the fans, the opposition and the ref. He wasn't expecting that!'

Maybe such motivational techniques will catch on.

Manchester United's stars must already be trembling at the prospect of Alex Ferguson in a G-string, stockings and suspenders.

The manager has to be an expert at coaxing his hungover stars out of bed and even preventing them from drinking on the morning of a game. *Time Out*'s Andrew Mosby once recorded a classic monologue from Marble Hill boss Phil (a cigar-smoking boss described as Mel Smith meets Terry Venables). He confronted his errant players with the immortal: 'How can you drink beer at this time of the morning, you sickos? I better buy a bottle of Scotch.'

How does the boss attain his coveted position? Usually it's because he's the loudest person in the pub and no other sod will do it. 'Our manager Dude was appointed because he's eighteen stone overweight, bosses everyone about and knows everybody in Reading,' says Simon Davies of the Sun FC. 'He's like a benevolent dictator. If he goes to a party then everyone goes, and if he drops a player there's never any answering back.'

Dude is a British Rail employee, so he is used to being hated – asking for penalty fares and telling the winger he's on the bench can't be much different. He's another manager with a sartorial flourish, favouring half-mast jeans exposing a Dagenham cleavage, and a Reading bobble hat for match days, as he incites his lads to, 'Remember that arsehole at number eleven last week? Well, ignore this lot like you ignored him, and don't get in any hassles.'

Of course, it's in the manager's sanctum, the dressing room, that the real work is done. Graham Boase, the manager of A3 Milan, believes in the high-tech approach. 'He brought back a portable whiteboard from the US and in the dressing room he draws arrows and formations to show us who's playing in the hole, and always tells us "this is the most important game of your lives" before every match,' explains A3 Milan's Matthew Coulbeck.

A more timid style of man-management is recalled by George Ward of Milldean, who has fond memories of a former manager nicknamed 'the Corpse', because of his deathly pallor.

'He couldn't pick a team to save his life. He used to name the team in the dressing room and then run out of the room until all the arguments about who was playing where had stopped. He had to come on for five minutes in one game and nearly broke a leg – after that he never played or managed again.'

Foreign coaches often bring their own unique training methods with them. The now-defunct West Coast Armadillos were early recruits to the current fad of recruiting continental coaches like Arsène Wenger, Christian Gross and Ruud Gullit. Yes, they once had a Czechoslovakian gaffer. 'He claimed to have played with the great Hungarian, Puskas, in the fifties,' recalls Arthur Duke, suspecting a few Eastern European porkies. 'One evening at training he brought along some tennis balls. He said that if Puskas learnt to play controlling a tennis ball then so could we. We were useless with them and the manager took a lot of abuse.'

An alternative to the overweight pub 'character' as manager is the fitness fanatic. Duke recalls another former supremo: 'Basically, he was a forty-year-old divorcee filling his time constructively. He was always immaculately groomed and incredibly fit. He'd take us on long-distance runs and he'd never even be out of breath. He tried new training methods such as aerobics, he had us wrapping our hands around our heads and his favourite phrase was "hate the opposition not each other". But then he remarried and quit in disgust after we lost 6-1. We went on to win the cup.'

On match days, the manager should spend 90 minutes hollering, 'Foot on the ball' or, 'Put 'im under!', but some hard-pressed bosses have to concentrate on several tasks at once. 'One opposition manager had a linesman's flag in one hand and a mobile phone in the other. He was taking calls from his mini-cab firm, barking instructions to his team and abusing us all at the same time,' recalls Duke.

Another manager of an East End side in the Maccabi Southern Football League had a notorious reputation. He was a taxi driver and his managerial technique owed more to Grant Mitchell than Arsène Wenger. After his tactical instructions were disobeyed once too often, he ran on the pitch and began brawling with one of his own players – who also happened to be his son.

The Sunday league gaffer is nothing if not inventive in his ways of communicating with the pitch. When the manager of Wiltshire side Ferndale Rodbourne YCFC was suspended and banned from the touchline, he stood on a hill overlooking the pitch and communicated with his assistant on the touchline with a two-way radio.

'You're all crap!'

The half-time team talk is when the manager can really get his clichés – sorry, tactical points – over to the lads. Lokomotiv manager Gary Birchall prefers the good old-fashioned rollicking. 'He does the Messiah and slams his hands on the ground in despair. He often explodes, and shouts, "You're all crap!"' says Brian Benson. Birchall receives the traditional response from the Sunday league footballer. 'We all just take the piss out of him,' says Benson.

'At least we can understand Gary though. One of our former managers, Dave Lucas, was always talking about 'not getting sucked in' and no one ever knew what he was talking about. He completely bamboozled us. He'd say "play to the percentages" or "use the channels", and he tried a diamond formation long before Glenn Hoddle made it popular, but we never understood a word of it.'

Managers are always in trouble for abusing their own players, the opposition and the fans. But ex-pat teams have an advantage when it comes to giving the opposition verbals. London side FC Porto has a mixture of English and Portuguese players, and manager Nelson Salsinha shouts from the touchline in a hybrid of cockney and Portuguese.

'He'll say something like "Pass the bolla!"' says Porto's Tony Carboso. 'He'll talk to the Portuguese in Portuguese and the rest in English. He tends to swear in Portuguese so the ref can't tell what he's saying. He'll shout in Portuguese: "Look at that big fat centre half who can't run and smells like he's been on the booze all night. He's twice your age and you forwards can't get past him!" It's just as well the opposition can't understand otherwise there might be a riot.'

Of course, managerial kidology can always backfire. Some managers can actually inspire their team to concede goals. Steve Hurst, a former star of the Civil Service FC, recalls the Czechoslovakian tour when the sixth-eleven manager Micky Cooper, a rotund Scotsman, was drafted into emergency goalkeeping service and somehow kept his goal intact. 'He gave us hell and kept calling himself "Clean Sheet Cooper" over the mike on the coach for the next three days. So, in the next game, when the Czechs did finally score against him, our bench erupted. The opposition thought we were completely mad.'

And the most advanced tactical realignments from the touchline can be ruined by the most unexpected of events. Philip Bird of Nottingham's Duke of Wellington side takes up the story: 'The manager gave a ten-minute detailed team talk on who was to pick up the opposition centre forward and so on. We had two subs and the manager was shouting his usual tactical instructions from the touchline. Only, after twenty minutes the referee counted up the players and told him that we only had ten players on the pitch. No one had noticed! He didn't half look embarrassed. It was 0-0 at the time and we went on to lose 5-1 with eleven players.'

Getting a result on Sunday can lead the unlikeliest of figures into temptation. You'd think that having a policeman in charge of your side would minimise the chances of corruption. But no. There's a famous tale of one Sunday league side in the north-east that had to win to stay up. At half-time they were 2-0 down and the opposition's star player was performing superbly. Somehow the lads had to put him out of the game. Help arrived at half-time from the unlikeliest of sources – a police patrol car. Two officers got out of the car and took the opposition's stunned star player away for questioning.

The side's manager, a member of the Old Bill himself, had arranged for the police to take him away on some minor charge. Strangely, the 'suspect' was innocent, and after helping the police with their inquiries was allowed to return home without charge, but long after the game had finished. The policeman's side then went on to win 3-2. Whenever the players of certain clubs have a few beers, the story still comes out. Other policemen get twenty years for aiding international drug smugglers; this policeman risked everything for a place in the middle echelons of a minor Sunday league.

Yes, it's a multi-faceted role being a club supremo in the 1990s, involving slick PR skills in the local pub, a knowledge of sports nutrition (Lucozade followed by beer and crisps), sporting psychology ('Give 110 per cent lads!') and a total lack of fashion sense. The next time you see a lonely figure in half-mast trousers pacing the touchline, desperately trying to coax the number nine out of bed on his mobile phone, don't call the police – he's a football manager.

MANAGER SPEAK

Put 'im under!

You're getting sucked in!

Remember the three Cs!

Keep it tight for the first fifteen!

Get your face on this!

Play it down the channels!

Short balls to feet!

Deep breaths!

This is the most important game of your lives!

Hit 'em hard!

Get your tackles in first!

Push right on the line!

Hate the opposition, not yourselves!

Just keep battling!

Whatever you do, do it with a smile on your face!

It's all about attitude!

Next tackle!

You're all crap!

MANAGER WEAR (pick and mix from)

Stockings and suspenders

Scuffed leather jacket

Tracksuit (dayglo colours obligatory)

Alex Ferguson padded jacket

Anorak

Suit

WW1 trenchcoat

Half-mast jeans

Brian Clough sweatshirt

Bobble hat

Baseball cap

Gloves

Doctor Who scarf

Scuffed trainers

ACCESSORIES

Mobile phone

Bottle of Scotch

Can of Tennant's

Portable whiteboard

Cigarettes

Cigar

Half-time oranges

Hipflask

Tennis balls (if Czechoslovakian)

Result cards

List of phone numbers

Linesman's flag

P45

Arthur Cresswell: Parkside FC

If mickey-taking is a sign of affection in football, then 66-year-old Parkside boss Arthur Cresswell is a very popular man. He's nicknamed 'Jimmy Savile' by the lads on account of his dayglo tracksuits, purchased every year on the club tour of Holland. 'He's got a dorsal fin one, and one that looks like a banana. And his cap's sewn to his head!' explains left back Kip Cross. 'When he takes it off his hair comes off too!' adds another player, to uproarious laughter.

At this point Cresswell himself emerges from his van, clad in a flame-strewn tracksuit. 'That's right, have your laugh now, before the dressing room,' says the taciturn boss, who's been compared to Kenny Dalglish by his players: 'He doesn't say much, and what he does say you can't understand.'

Every player has his tale of Arthur's single-minded approach to Wimbledon and District League side Parkside. 'If it doesn't concern football he's not interested. You'll phone up and say something like, "My dad's just died", and he'll say, "Does that mean you can't play, then?" Or if you say you've got to go to a wedding he'll moan, "Can't they get married in the summer?"' reveals Cross.

But on the pitch the joking stops and the lads would die for Cresswell. Parkside are based in Merton, south London. They have a phenomenal record under Arthur's stewardship, winning 27 trophies in seventeen years. In 1996 the side clocked up its fourth successive championship, breaking a league record of 36 years standing.

Arthur is a legend at Parkside. For eighteen years he's been both manager and secretary: the bloke who collects the subs, gets the kit washed, organises club tours to Holland, spends £200 of his own money on trophies for the end-of-season awards bash and runs the line each week. He never takes money from the club for phone calls, stamps or half-time drinks.

Arthur has such high standards, he makes Kenny Dalglish seem loquacious. 'He's not very happy when we win, so you can imagine what he's like when we lose,' quips Kip Cross. 'He did just about smile when we won the cup last year,' adds midfielder James Tobin. There are no Barry Fry-style jigs down the touchline from Cresswell. While running the line, the closest he comes to emotion is lighting a fag when the lads are 5-0 up.

When he isn't working as a driver for Mercedes Benz, Cresswell lives, breathes, eats, sleeps and dreams Parkside FC. 'It helps keep me young,' he says. 'I wake up at eight o'clock on Saturday morning and the adrenaline starts to flow. I start checking the kit and then I can't get to the ground quick enough. It's only when all the boys are here that I can relax. I hate the close season. I'm just left kicking my heels.

'Luckily my wife Eve is also very dedicated to football – she's

washing the kits until ten o'clock every Saturday night.' Before
one cup tie, long-suffering Eve was up until the small hours due
to the lads' Klinsmann dive routines. The kit needed four
washes. And as for Arthur's son, Mark, well, he shares his
father's enthusiasm, being captain of Parkside.

Arthur is the first man at the ground. An hour and a half
before kick-off he takes out the corner flags, collecting them at
the end of the game. Every week each player finds his shirt,
shorts, socks and tracksuit top all neatly folded in polythene
bags and laid out in the dressing room. 'They say I moan a lot,
but I've one lad who says he could never play for anyone else,
because he wouldn't get his kit in a polythene bag,' says Arthur.

The shirts all have PFC written across their backs. Each shirt
and tracksuit top has a badge based around a park motif with
the club's motto, '*Facta Non Verba*' (Deeds Not Words),
inevitably thought up by Arthur, underneath.

'Being an ex-army man I believe in doing and not talking
about it,' says Cresswell, sounding, at least to his irreverent
players, more than a little like Foggy from *Last of the Summer
Wine*. 'I say to the players, "When you go out there, remember
what kit you're wearing. Look at the motto of the shirt you're
putting on and remember it." That motto is one of the reasons
we're so successful.'

Arthur could mount his own version of *The Generation
Game* with his matchday gear. He's got everything except the
cuddly toy. 'He brings about six bags of kit with him to each
game, including the kit, hooded tops, first aid, ball bag with
football pump, a bag of isotonic drinks, subs jackets, water bag
and sponge,' says Jimmy Tobin. And if that isn't enough,
Arthur, a former referee, is linesman for every match. Then for
the rest of the week he's busy on his computer, keeping
Parkside addresses, results, fixtures, income and expenditure
records up to date.

It's hard to believe that back in 1978, during Arthur's first
game in charge, Parkside lost 10-0. He immediately set about
rebuilding the side and improving standards and by his second
season trophies came to the club. And he's even taken Parkside
into Europe, winning seventeen out of eighteen matches played.

'We're the best turned-out team in the league. Every player must wear his shirt inside his shorts with his socks pulled up,' explains James Tobin. 'I like to see my boys looking smart,' says Cresswell. It's paid dividends on the pitch. You sense the opposition are intimidated as soon as they see Parkside warming up in their professional tracksuit tops with the club's name on the back.

Although Arthur regularly threatens to retire after a defeat, you sense he'll be an institution at Parkside for some time yet, inspiring the lads with lines like, 'If they haven't got the ball they can't score!' and, 'We're all in the same-colour shirt, so play for each other!'

Arthur is a master of touchline motivation. 'He always comes out with, "If you're tired, lads, keep breathing!"' says Jimmy Tobin. 'If he comes out with it we just laugh and think, We know that, Arf. If we didn't breathe we'd be dead. He doesn't have any secret hand signals, although he does have a special gesture after a good tackle, where he clenches his fist and swings it back and forward.'

Understandably, Arthur has a quiet pride in his achievements. 'We had Brian Gayle, the former Wimbledon player, as guest at one of our awards ceremonies,' recalls Arthur. 'He saw the huge trophies we were presenting and he said we were better organised than some League clubs he'd played for.'

With Parkside now playing in a higher division, Cresswell is still responding to new challenges. Meanwhile, the Arthur anecdotes will continue to flourish. Kip Cross remembers one phone call when he asked Arthur if he'd had a good Christmas. 'He said, "Yes. Can you play then?" And that was it! He's a great geezer, though. We think he must have Parkside tattooed on his backside!'

'I could go on all day about the amount of work he does. Arthur hasn't missed a match or a league meeting in eighteen years,' adds Tobin. 'We think he's the best bloke in football.'

Andy Gillies: Saracens Athletic FC

Bill Shankly, Alex Ferguson, Kenny Dalglish, George Graham, Andy Gillies . . . All great Scottish managers. Except in the case

of Andy Gillies, 34-year-old manager of Saracens Athletic in the
Coventry Sunday Combination League. He's not quite as
Scottish as he'd like to be.

'Andy says all great managers are Scottish and he'll talk
about himself, Ferguson and Dalglish in the same breath,'
explains Saracens midfielder and secretary Richard Macdonald.
'Andy comes from a family of nine, but the funny thing is that
he's the only one actually born in England. We call him "the
Plastic Jock" which really winds him up.'

'I definitely think of myself as Scottish,' explains Andy
himself. 'I'm related to Matt Gillies, manager of Leicester in the
1960s. The lads didn't believe me until they saw him on Sky the
other night.'

Another dressing-room moniker of 'Haggis' stuck with
Gillies after an unfortunate tour to Portobello in Scotland. 'It
was my most embarrassing moment ever,' remembers Andy. 'I
was in this chip shop with a Manchester United fan we call
"Rantona". I said, "You must try the haggis in batter." The
woman behind the counter said, "That's not haggis, it's black
pudding." Rantona was doubled up, shouting, "You call
yourself a Jock!" The lads ended up throwing me in the sea, but
I dried off in the pub.'

But, like his Scottish heroes, AG, as the lads call him, has
achieved great results with his club. During his four years in
charge, they've won two championships and two cups. The 5 ft
2 ins Gillies did play one game in goal for Saracens, but despite
winning 4-3, Andy says, 'The lads demanded we change a
winning team and I drop out. It must have been when I was
lobbed from 40 yards.' Richard Macdonald goes further: 'He
can't play to save his life.'

Management is much more AG's forte. His tactical nous is
renowned. 'I've tried playing the Christmas-tree formation. It
worked for the first ten minutes but after that it looked more
like a bush,' laughs Gillies.

Andy is famous at Saracens for his huge flasks: 'My current
flask holds 24 cups of tea or coffee, which is useful for
hangovers.'

'We reckon AG's flask is more reliable than most of us

players. He can never get it right though. Half the lads want tea, half want coffee, and he never puts enough sugar in it,' chips in Saracens defender Scott Drew.

'Sometimes I think they'd prefer a crate of lager,' sighs Andy.

Another Gillies motivational trick is his man-of-the-match award. Andy doesn't just present the same trophy week after week – he buys a new trophy every single match at his own expense.

'AG announced that through lack of commitment this will be his last season. That's why he'd introduced the man-of-the-match trophy – to make it a memorable way to go out,' says Scott Drew. 'Nobody believes him though, as every season is going to be his last. I'll put money on AG being around for years.'

Gillies did manage to win the man-of-the-match award himself one week, though. The referee gave it to Andy for his constant motivation from the touchline. 'I deserved it. The lads were crap that day,' says Andy.

Andy also pays for the kit washing out of his own pocket. 'I suggested at the start of the season when we were all skint, that as we were penniless we should all take our turn to wash the kit and save the £5 we paid his wife Margaret for the kit wash,' says Richard Macdonald. 'Andy's reply was, "Nobody can do the kit better than the wife. As long as she thinks the club are giving her something for doing the job, I'll sort her out with the money."'

The Saracens supremo showed typical Scottish shrewdness when he decided that too many footballs were being lost. He started saving cigarette tokens from the numerous fags he smokes during matches and sent off for a free ball. 'The wife does a cleaning job, so she started looking for old fag packets too. We had to get hundreds of them.'

'When the ball arrived it was like a balloon and lasted about twenty minutes,' reveals Scott Drew. 'Andy's always collecting for something free. He's a typical Jock.' Andy's famous free football was, of course, another source of infinite stick.

Andy works for a car component firm. The job isn't particularly well paid and he's on a short-term contract – but there was one managerial imposition Andy was not prepared to stand for. When a rush order came in, all staff were ordered to work Sunday morning shifts. 'I said I'd do Saturday, Sunday afternoon, anything but Sunday morning. They said I had to turn up, but I didn't and they gave me a written warning,' Gillies says disbelievingly.

'He was in complete shock as to why his company didn't understand that he has commitments on a Sunday morning,' remembers Richard Macdonald. Gillies is still dismayed that the vulgar world of commerce should be allowed to interfere with football: 'Work is work and football is football. Football comes first.'

The job has its perks, though. Like another great Scottish manager, Gillies is happy to accept the odd unsolicited gift. 'If we have a good game the lads don't half get me pissed!'

'We think he should be given the job for life,' says Richard Macdonald. 'We take his man-of-the-match awards for granted, a bit like Andy himself. But his commitment to the team is unquestioned, even to the point of madness.'

Under Andy Gillies it can only be a matter of time before the Saracens replace Coventry City as the region's premier side – but then again, according to one of his players, Andy also thinks that Scotland can win the World Cup.

10 And Pigs Might Fly

Outside the Flying Pig, a chalk-message board reads, 'Sod's Law: Anything that can go wrong does go wrong. Cole's Law: Grated cabbage and carrot.' Another sign reads, 'Happy Birthday Tom from the Pig. Welcome to the geriatric centre backs' club.'

It's 9.45 on Sunday morning and the Pig squad are sleepily assembling in the pub, building up to the game with coffee and a copy of the *Sunday Sport*. The bar is dimly lit with only the flashing lights of the fruit machines challenging damaged craniums. There's a dreamy atmosphere of blokeish camaraderie peculiar to the morning after a night in the pub.

'Smiley' Dave Smith is pinning up his match report from last week's game, a 4-2 victory over Lode. Every club has someone like Smiley, the player who indulges his literary fancies in tongue-in-cheek match reports. Smiley is clearly a frustrated novelist and will perhaps one day do for Cambridge what Graham Swift did for Fenland, by writing the great Mortgage Quest League Cup Round Three novel: 'Heavy clouds rolled in, behind which a brilliant sun found chinks through which to spotlight individual players. An eerie silence descended over the amassed hordes of the Pig Army and refused to lift, despite the best efforts of the more vocally liberated.'

At the end of the match report, there's even a list of players' appearances, goals and bookings, more comprehensive than some Premiership programmes. There is also a list of enough sponsors to satisfy even Manchester United: 'Flying Pig are kindly sponsored by Greg Middleton, members of the London Stock Exchange. Half-time oranges generously supplied courtesy of Hilary's Wholesale. Medical equipment supplied courtesy of Big Rich Enterprises and Stratagene.'

Morale is as high as it ever gets early on a Sunday morning with the Pig three points clear at the top of Division 2B of the Cambridge and District Sunday League. A fleet of battered cars ferries the squad to the Cambridge stadium. It's a compact, well-kept ground, with a neat black clubhouse and a new wire perimeter fence around it, preventing the usual ball-in-the-river scenario. It's used by the league for cup finals and has been rented after astute negotiations by Smiley and Co. On winter mornings, the wind whistles across the pitch from the Fens.

Walking through the car park is Jimmy 'Seventies Man' Cameron, aka The Student. He has Supergrass sideburns and is wearing a knee-length seventies sheepskin coat and flares, looking like something from an episode of *Starsky and Hutch*. He used to play for West Ham's youth team and joined the Pig while at Cambridge University. He's now studying archaeology at Bournemouth, which is perhaps why he looks like a piece of history himself. It's a mark of the devotion that the Pigs inspire that Seventies Man has commuted from the south coast for this crunch game against Babraham, the second-placed side in the division. Not many sides can travel back in time to make loan signings from three decades ago.

'It's The Student!' hollers a team-mate. 'What are you doing here? Has your grant run out? You must have taken a loan out to get up here!'

The lads are changing when the inevitable latecomer arrives. He walks in wearing a bright orange shirt with a sparkling medallion underneath. 'Fucking hell, it's a cross between Tango Man and Medallion Man!' quips a club wit. Tango Man is Kevin Diver aka Mr Cadbury's Parrot – because, according to club secretary Joanne Griffiths, 'He shouts "Kevin Diver!" when he goes up for a header and he sounds like a parrot.'

Jimmy Cameron is feeling nervous, which you don't expect from someone who looks like he's been playing since 1971. 'I was dreaming of free-kick routines last night,' he confesses.

'Look, I can't take you seriously in that gear,' laughs Michael 'Wacko' Jackson, the manager. 'Can I have that coat?'

Cameron stands before the mirror, removes a ring from his

pierced eyebrow and places a plaster over it. 'What winks and shags like a tiger?' quips a team-mate.

Wacko announces the team. 'Nursey is in goal,' he announces (Stewart Cousins' new nickname is the result of the manager's fancy dress party). He then names the rest of the side before ending with, 'Jules and The Student up front.'

After a professional-looking bout of stretching on the touchline, the lads return to the dressing room for their team talk. Mike Jackson is a scouser who looks like Steve McMahon. His trusted lieutenant Russell, one of the club's founders, stands alongside him. They are both wearing the club's 'Baby Gro' sub suits, which look not unlike the sort of thing you'd put your one-year-old in.

Wacko's face is resolute. 'Right, I shouldn't have to motivate you for this. It's the most important game of the season and you've gotta fucking want it!' Wacko is the Brian Little of the Sunday league, oozing commitment and earnestness. His face is creased in grim commitment. This is serious stuff. He looks more like a Premiership manager than most Premiership managers. 'If we win we can go six points clear at the top. We've got to match them for work rate and commitment. Get the ball down and look for your man. Luke, make yourself available on the right. You've done fucking great this season and if you win this one you've got a chance of winning it. Let's fucking want this!'

A collective cheer and cries of 'Come on, lads!' go up from the players as they leave the dressing room with the familiar clatter of studs on lino.

Bringing home the bacon

As the game kicks off, around twenty people are gathered on the touchline. Club secretary Joanne Griffiths, who lives with keeper Stewart Cousins, is on the clubhouse balcony with their baby son Jack, the Pig's youngest supporter. She and four other players' partners discuss events in last night's taxi queue.

On the touchline, Smiley is wearing black leather strides. He's 'reserve team coach' as well as the barman at the Flying

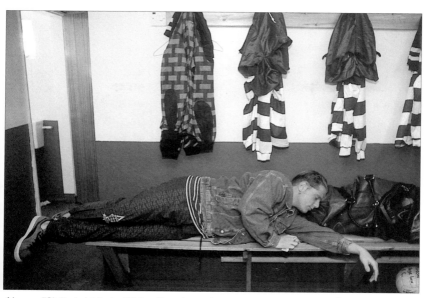

Above "S'all right lads, I'll be fine, just give me the . . . urrrrgh!" *(Mark Pinder)*

Below Parkside salute boss Arthur Cresswell *(Mark Pain)*

Above Mad Dog waits to come on *(Mark Pinder)*

Left Andy Gillies, Scottish supremo, sweeper and all round dogsbody at Saracens *(Jason Tilley)*

Top right Sunday league football at its sartorial finest *(Allsport)*

Bottom right Grace, style, balance, skill . . . but not in this game *(Mark Pain)*

Above "Referee! . . . Referee! . . . I said Referee!! . . . Oh forget it!" *(John Gichigi, Allsport)*

Left The ball went that way . . . *(Mark Pain)*

Top right New Dutch signing Van Hire makes an instant impact *(John Super)*

Bottom right "We'll have the ball out of the river just as soon as we find a long stick, lads . . ." *(John Super)*

Above "Right, we're bringing the toddlers on . . ." Chiarina Fernandez gees up the Trafalgar Colts *(John Anderson)*

Below A half-time isotonic fag *(Allsport)*

If God hadn't meant football to be played in the air, he'd never have invented Sunday league *(Allsport)*

"Oi ref, you need glasses!" *(Allsport)*

Ravanelli, as he might look in 20 years time *(Allsport)*

Above The boss goes mental, the lads ignore him *(John Gichigi, Allsport)*

Top right Bringing home the bacon: the Flying Pigs' Joanne Griffiths and Stewart Cousins *(Andrew Parsons)*

Bottom right Glad to be grey: even your grandad can get a game in goal *(Alex Livesey, Allsport)*

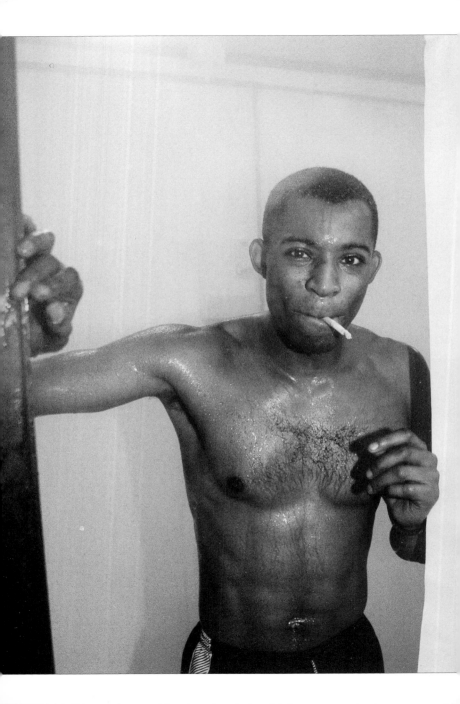

Left Keeping it clean: "I just wash, smoke and go . . ." *(Andrew Parsons)*

Right Don't look now mate, but that's hair remover *(Andrew Parsons)*

Below Arthur Cresswell wins Parkside's coveted bad taste tracksuit award *(Mark Pain)*

Above Quiet after-match reflection upon a six-pint fixture *(Mark Pinder)*

Below It's the author's turn to wash the kit *(Allsport)*

Above Paul Kettel and the Crazy Gang's luxury match-day coach *(Windy Millers)*

Below Bash Street Kids: The Windy Millers as Dennis the Menace *(Windy Millers)*

Left A very Windy Miller: Fat Lane loses his pants *(Windy Millers)*

Below Blue Moon: in a bottom of the table clash it's Arse'n'all 11 Windy Millers 0 (*Windy Millers*)

Pig. 'You should watch out for Jimmy,' he advises, 'and Colin once reached the quarter-finals of the FA Vase.'

Also on the sidelines is club Old Spice Ian 'Zico' Reid. He's the oldest player at the club at 47, and was playing for the first team until he was 45. 'I'm so old they presented me with a plastic dinosaur at the alternative awards.'

Also present is club president Julian. It's not a taxing role for the 40-something Pig aficionado: 'All I have to do is buy a round,' he explains. Other reserves and opposition fans make up the crowd. It's a well-run club and there's even a man in the clubhouse selling tea and coffee to the spectators.

Sadly there is no appearance of fans Flip-Flop Phil and Mags, despite a rare sighting the previous week. As Smiley put it in his match report: 'For the first time in FPFC's history, the Flying Pig's answer to Mulder and Scully, in matching FBI raincoats, turned up to spectate. The normally nocturnal pairing are never usually seen during daylight hours and perhaps it was the gloom caused by the heavy cloud cover that allowed them to venture out without being turned into a pillar of salt.'

The club's maddest supporter, Big Rich, is now working in Amsterdam, but returns whenever he can, sporting a flying helmet and giant pig's ears. He is Big Rich Enterprises – sponsor of the medical bag.

It's not going well on the pitch. The early chances all fall to Babraham.

'Talkin', boys! Talkin'!' yells Wacko, pacing the line in his boiler suit while sipping a cup of steaming coffee.

Keeper Stewart Cousins rescues the side in several one-on-one situations while Babraham miss a number of inviting chances. A lob goes inches past the post. As Wacko becomes more animated, his accent becomes more scouse.

'Win the header, eh? Come on, dig in, let's raise it! Let's get a Pig head on this!'

Jimmy goes on a jinking run and shoots just wide to calm the Pig fans' nerves a little. Then a bizarre shout of 'Woodwork!' goes up from all eleven Pig players when Babraham hit the post. This is for the benefit of Joanne Griffiths, who's compiling the stats for the club 'Swindle' sweepstake, where for a pound each, the players bet on the first shot to hit the woodwork, first throw in, first booking, etc.

'Where's the shape? Luke, use the force!' shouts a spectator at midfielder Luke. But the empire strikes back. In the 37th minute, Babraham finally take the lead. The mood slumps. 'There is a shape. It's pear-shaped,' adds the fan.

At half-time the players slump on to the dressing-room benches. Stewart Cousins is puffing at an isotonic fag. Mike Jackson needs all his powers of motivation.

'We could be 7-1 down but the point is we got away with it. Just settle down and believe in yourselves. They're a yard quicker in thought and action. You're all capable of passing it. Just lay it five yards and keep possession. Frustrate them; don't go for the killer pass. I'm going to change it around a little. We'll play a flat back four – Steve can go to left back and Luke to the right side of midfield. Simple passes, that's the name of the game.'

The Flying Pig miss a good chance straight from the kick-off. Then a Babraham forward called Roycey pierces the Pig offside trap again, rounds Stewart Cousins and taps the ball into the unguarded net. It looks all over. A few minutes later, Steve Gilbey is booked for a foul.

'Make it worth a booking next time,' shouts one of the fans.

The Pig then improve a little. The side hits the post and a good free-kick opportunity is blazed wide. At least the players are still smiling and joking with each other, something you never see in professional football. Zico agrees: 'Journalists who write about money killing the game should come down here. You'll never kill football. These people pay £3 a week to play for the love of it.'

Can we not nick it?

It's been a sporting game, but suddenly it's beset by enough controversy to have even John Motson searching through his annals. The Pig's Gilbey is sent off for another foul, his second bookable offence.

'You fucking cunt, ref!' hollers a spectator. The Pigs might not be flying, but the language is.

Then the ball goes over the top of the Pig defence as a massive cry of 'Offside!' goes up and the linesman flags. The ref waves play on. Two Babraham forwards rush through but contrive to put the chance just wide.

'You can't be offside from a goal kick,' says the ref.

The Pig players insist that it was a free kick. The ref blows the final whistle anyway.

'What a fucking cock-up!' says Tango Man as the players walk off the pitch.

The diminutive referee reaches for his book and announces, 'I am sending you off for foul and abusive language.'

And some people are on the pitch. Two red cards in the final three minutes on top of failing to bring home the bacon has proved too much for the Pig contingent. The ref is surrounded by players, managers and fans.

'Have you got something to say to me? If you have you can come here and say it,' fumes the ref at assistant manager Russell. 'I've had no alternative but to send him off for foul and abusive language to the referee.'

The general opinion is that the ref is, in the parlance of the Flying Pig, a right runt. Club president and linesman Julian has joined the mêlée.

'If you point that flag at me you'll be reported,' says the ref, sounding uncannily like the verger in *Dad's Army*.

The players retreat to the dressing room, cursing Men In Black, as the ref makes for his car.

'It didn't run for us, lads,' says Russell.

'We'll beat 'em back at their place,' adds Zico.

'There's a long way to go yet, lads,' consoles Mike Jackson.

Then a collective chorus of foul language goes up from the Pig dressing room.

'I don't fucking believe it! My wallet's gone!'

In fact, nearly everyone's valuables have gone.

'Who was last out? They should have locked the door . . .'

It's a Sunday-morning nightmare. Someone has forgotten to lock the changing room and seven wallets have gone missing on this Sunday bloody Sunday. Russell is instantly on the clubhouse phone, cancelling his cards. As Mr Blair said, things can only get better. There are numerous suspects, but no one has actually seen anyone enter the changing rooms. In truth, the thief has got away. Local youths have been going past the changing room all game, there were numerous strange faces in a sizeable crowd and there's even a so-called football writer up from London.

Yet fifteen minutes later, back at the pub, team spirit is being restored by pints all round bought by those left with cash. Joanne Griffiths is sitting down with baby Jack compiling the Swindle results and filling in the match details for the league. 'Jack came to the pub when he was one day old,' says dad Stewart proudly.

The Student is getting the usual stick from his team-mates. 'Did they put some money *in* your wallet, Jimmy? Who'd nick his wallet, eh? There's only a student union card in it.'

Tango Man is still complaining about his sending off. 'I didn't swear at him. I said, "It was a fucking cock-up." That was all.'

Gratis sausage and chips from the pub help everyone. Club founder Russell Dunne, a chartered surveyor, explains how the club started in 1991, based around a core of Cambridge Radio staff who drank in the Pig, and has progressed steadily ever since.

Russell's proudest moment was the lengthy debate with the league over a postponed Mortgage Quest League cup tie. The game was played after the pitch was cleared of water but the opposition complained that some of their players had gone home, believing the game had been postponed. The league ordered the game to be replayed.

Russell then turned barrister in defence of the Flying Pig, compiling Don Revie-like dossiers of evidence to take before two league meetings. But, despite his Rumpole-style perform-ance, and coverage in the local press, the game still had to be replayed and the Flying Pig lost. But it was a battle that Russell relished. 'I suppose I just have a strong sense of justice. My wife is a solicitor so that helped.'

A couple of pints later, the result of the Swindle is announced and Russell reads out the other results from the league to a mass of boos and cheers. The Student leaves for a rendezvous with

Huggy Bear. Tango Man has almost forgotten about his altercation with the referee and even Wacko lightens up.

It takes more than a home defeat, two sendings off and a robbery to keep down a Flying Pig, even though the players later learn that hundreds of pounds are being spent in Cambridge city centre while we drink. For once, 'We woz robbed' takes on a whole new meaning.

Stewart Cousins: Probably The Best Bloke In Football

In 1996, Stewart Cousins was declared the winner of the prestigious FC/Carlsberg Probably The Best Bloke In Football award. There aren't many people in Sunday league football who'd try to clear a waterlogged pitch with a bucket and sponge. But Stewart Cousins is not a man who's easily deterred. The prospect of a postponed Mortgage Quest League cup tie involving his beloved Flying Pig was too much for Cousins to tolerate. The game had been postponed at 8.30 am, but 22 players were there and the referee said the game could go ahead if some of the water was cleared.

Stewart went out on to the pitch with a fork, digging holes to remove the excess water. This was a man who clearly did give a fork for his club. After a lengthy period of forking hell he then, to the general disbelief of the team, took out a sponge and bucket and began mopping up the excess water. 'The lads thought I was mad. They wouldn't help; there was just me mopping with the sponge, and the club linesman with a paper cup, and then I put sawdust on the treated areas,' recalls Stewart, who is no longer a fan of Wet Wet Wet.

Every team needs someone like Cousins, who's either a diamond geezer, complete mug or man in need of psychiatric help, depending on what line you take on football devotion to the point of obsession. The 31-year-old Cousins has only been at the Cambridge and District Sunday League club for four years, but has already made himself indispensable. He was an able goalkeeper during the Flying Pig's 1994–95 promotion season, but, during a goal famine, as official 'Club Tall Person', he was happy to utilise his six foot six inches up front and scored six goals. Then came disaster. In the final game of the season, he was carried off and underwent an operation to reconstruct his cruciate ligament – but is now back in the side as flying custodian.

When he was out of the side through injury, he kept himself busy as the club treasurer, trainer, first-aid man, kit manager, match-ball washer and half-time orange and water bottle provider. 'His bag is bottomless,' says midfielder Colin Jobling. 'You wouldn't believe what he's got in it. Tape, scissors, strappings, spare studs, tie-ups, spare laces, spare goalie's gloves and shorts. Everything you could ever think of.'

His partner, club secretary Joanne Griffiths, had been at the club for nine months when finally their eyes met across a crowded fixture list and they decided to spend more half-times with each other.

'On our first date we met for a quick drink at lunchtime and ended up talking about football all afternoon,' recalls Stewart, who is a fan of Cambridge United on Saturday afternoons. 'She's my ideal woman. She's as committed to football as I am and when the chairman offers to let us watch the games on Sky round at his house it's always Joanne that says yes.' It's clearly a satellite of love, as Lou Reed might have put it.

And there aren't even any kit-washing rows. 'I can't use the washing machine at weekends because Stewart is doing the kit. He's so methodical – he folds it all up neatly, which I never used to,' laughs Joanne.

Since Stewart took over as treasurer he has transformed the club's finances. 'The accounts were in disarray when he took over, but now we've got money in the bank,' says Dale Smith, who introduced Cousins to the club. His first step was to utilise his six foot six frame collecting subs.

'It's only £1.50 subs if you just play one half like I often do, but Stewart won't let it lie,' says Smith. 'He'll phone every five minutes, threaten to send the boys round or stand over you and then you only come up to his belly button. He wears you down and you end up paying.'

'I send them individual bills in the post. That usually shames them into paying,' adds Stewart.

His next step was to seek sponsorship. 'His dad's a local businessman. It took a lot of persuading and quite a few beers, but somehow Stewart persuaded him to sponsor the subs' tracksuits for £45 a season. Stewart then sewed on his dad's company logo himself,' says Joanne Griffiths. He then persuaded business contacts at the Cambridge United vice-presidents' club to sponsor match balls.

But Stewart still wasn't sure that the club's potential income was being maximised. Incredibly, he even found a sponsor for the club's half-time oranges. 'I work as a chef so I persuaded one of our vegetable suppliers, Matt Gray, to donate the oranges. In return he gets a namecheck in the club newsletter. And a mate of mine at Britvic has donated some water containers too.'

Cousins can persuade anyone to do just about anything for the Flying Pig. When the side played away games near his parents' and sister's homes, he talked them into providing free half-time tea and bacon sandwiches for the supporters.

As well as helping with fund-raising events like the end-of-season awards party, summer barbecues, a Halloween disco and Christmas draw, Stewart also introduced the Swindle Sweepstake. Last season it raised £400 for the club. Each Sunday, Stewart can be heard engaging in frenzied Swindle arguments over the time of the first foul or the first shot to hit the woodwork.

'When Stewart goes into something, he goes into it 100 per cent. He makes sure he knows his stuff,' says Dale Smith. 'He's got a photographic memory. He can tell you how many points we've got, what position we're in. He knows every ground and every player. He's pretty cute when it comes to beer too. He knows exactly who owes him a drink.'

Stewart's ideal weekend involves training with the Flying Pig from Thursday to Saturday (i.e. drinking in the pub every night), watching Cambridge United on Saturdays and playing for the Flying Pig on Sundays followed by a good game on Sky.

This can lead to mood swings, reveals Joanne. 'If the Flying Pig lose he's a complete pain to live with. After the game he'll chuck his water bottles around and walk up to the goalkeeper and say, "Can you talk me through that one again?" I can tell if the lads have lost by the way he throws his bag down.'

Now he's back in goal, Stewart will still bring his bottomless bag to games – 'If I didn't bring these things no one else would' – and carry on his off-pitch organising. 'The club would fall apart without him,' says Dale Smith. 'Once he had to miss a game because he was working and we had nothing at all. We even forgot the balls.'

Cousins' commitment even extends to penning a musical accolade to the Flying Pig. 'I wrote this song for the supporters and sang it all night. It went, "We are black, we are white, we are fucking dynamite/Ooh, oink, oink, aah!" The barman threatened to ban me if I sang it one more time.'

Stewart Cousins – he really is the bloke who makes Pigs fly. And just to prove it, after receiving his Best Bloke award at London's Waldorf Hotel, he and Joanne invited the rest of the club round to watch Euro 96, placed the cans of Carlsberg in a bin in the middle of the room, and proceeded to drink a year's supply of beer in a matter of days. 'Ooh, oink, oink, aah!' indeed.

11 A Right Shower

Sunday league shower scenes are more horrific than anything Alfred Hitchcock could have filmed in *Psycho*. If Norman Bates's mother had bought a motel in England and signed up young Norm for the local footie side, film history would have been forever changed. Bates would never have wanted to enter a shower again and Janet Leigh would have been able to just wash and go.

Every side has its tale of showers that are invariably ferociously hot or chillingly cold, or, even worse, hot for ten minutes and then veer to gonad-shrinking temperatures. It starts off with the horrible sensation of bare feet on cold tiles and ends in naked men with red flesh forming a human pyramid trying to reach a red wheel that looks like a prop from *Doctor Who*. Some days it's apparently welded in one position. On other mornings the shower wheel simply falls off. Or if it is movable, the lads turn it to blue and the showers get hotter; if they turn it to red they get colder. And always some showers emit a pathetic trickle and others a torrent.

Every local council in the land must spend huge sums employing men to make furtive visits to their changing rooms early on Sunday mornings to sabotage the showers and ensure they're at the wrong temperature. It's no coincidence that Irvine Welsh made a cameo appearance in the TV film of *The Granton Star Cause* playing a council worker in the parks fending off complaints about the inoperative showers from Granton Star FC.

But despite its variable quality, the shower is still the great bonding place of Sunday football. Every week it's the same. Once the initial moaning about the game is over, talk turns to

Saturday's football results, the after-match choice of pubs, the Sky game and how the number nine got those scratches on his back. Mud-strewn kit, shin pads, tie-ups and jockstraps are discarded in a collective heap on the floor. The on-pitch animosity is soon forgotten as all 22 players unite in a shared goal of far greater importance – how to get the bloody thing to work.

That after-match shower produces its own distinctive characters. There is the player who always forgets his shampoo, the farter figure who can clear a packed shower in ten seconds, and the star who always cleans his boots in there, resulting in flood scenes reminiscent of coastal Bangladesh. 'We always have blocked drains and we end up wallowing in four inches of muddy water,' sighs Martin Bester of the Masons Arms in Yeovil.

Beneath the spurting nozzles is the ideal territory for the practical joker. A few years ago a Sunday league footballer phoned up Simon Mayo's 'confessions' spot to admit that he once put hair remover in a team-mate's shampoo. It was going hilariously well until the opposition's ape-like centre half asked if he could borrow the shampoo too. The joker made a rapid retreat and developed a mysterious injury for the return fixture.

'We have one lad who's a nutter. He waits by the showers and douses a different player with the trainer's bucket of cold water each week,' says Bill Liddiard of Swindon side Jesters. 'His aim is to soak the entire squad by the end of the season.'

Then there is the player who never showers. 'Often it's the younger players,' says Martin Bester. 'They've just come from schoolboy football and are a bit bashful in front of all these hairy-arsed blokes.' Other players simply scarper early to avoid paying their subs or taking their turn washing the kit.

Not having a shower does have some historical precedents. Martin Broughton, the former secretary of Signcroft, points out that 'in the good old days the pubs used to close at 2 pm on Sunday'. Kick-offs were inevitably late, and by the time he'd taken down the nets and rounded up the kit, it was dangerously near closing time. So obviously it was straight into the pub without a shower. 'There was also the added pleasure of leaving a trail of drying mud all over the pub carpet,' adds Broughton.

Stewart Cousins of the Flying Pig in Cambridge has one player who plays on both Saturdays and Sundays: 'He refuses to shower after the Saturday game as he says he'll only get dirty again the next day. There are always a couple who just daub on the anti-perspirant and then go straight down the pub.

'Mind you, once we had a game that was postponed and one of our lads still took a shower as he said he'd promised his wife that he'd come home clean for once.'

In the professional world, players celebrate in the showers too, although presumably they don't clean their boots in them. Vinny Jones once marked a Wimbledon victory by dancing naked while smoking a cigar in the Manchester United showers. He also turned his ghetto blaster up full volume so that the dejected United players could hear it next door. And when John Beck was manager at Cambridge he decided that the players would benefit from a cold shower before the game and chucked cold water over the likes of Dion Dublin in an unusual attempt at liquid motivation.

But at Sunday league level, showers – or lack of them – are frequently used as a tactical weapon. 'We have a deliberate policy of using a pitch that doesn't have showers or changing rooms,' says Richard Macdonald of Saracens in Coventry. 'The other sides are always pissed off at having to use that pitch, so it gives us an advantage before a ball is kicked. Our bunch of dirty bastards are quite happy to get changed in their cars and then go straight down the pub after the game. We all wake up on Monday morning with muddy knees and mud crumbs all over the bed.'

Ah, the mud crumbs in the bed routine. Many a relationship must have been ruined by that horrible crunchy feeling, just as you've settled down for the night. Although the man could never be accused of lying – all along he said he liked a woman who was dirty in bed.

'I played for one team where we didn't have showers,' remembers the Flying Pig's Stewart Cousins. 'We just took it in turns to rub ourselves down with the trainer's bucket and sponge.' That's one team you could never make a soap opera about.

The Sunday league shower can even result in near fatalities. 'There's one village team in our league that is notorious for its showers,' says Martin Bester. 'One isn't earthed properly and you get a bolt from it. We think it's a deliberate ploy to kill the opposition off.'

Hugh Jones of Perfidious Albion remembers a particularly atrocious set of showers on some pitches near Brick Lane, London. 'There are three pitches there and the showers have about five heads. It's atrocious – all the teams that have played there before sprint off at the end to get to the showers. And of course the first five players go in in their boots and clean them in the shower. So whoever eventually gets in after queuing up with 59 other players ends up in something like the Somme.'

Whatever the problems with showers, it's not often that the police get involved. But London's Philosophy Football side were nearly arrested after a game at Regent's Park. The team entered the showers after a heavy defeat. Only then a female jobsworth told the players that as it was after 4 pm and she wasn't getting paid, she was turning the water off. The players were left with wet mud trickling down their legs.

'One of the players turned them back on. We got back in, but then this middle-aged woman came in, oblivious to the fact that we were all naked, and turned the water off again,' remembers secretary Jeff Andrews.

'This happened a couple of times before two policemen arrived. We thought it was Jeremy Beadle. But then it turned out that they were the parks police and they gave us a long lecture on how lowly paid park staff are and told us to go home.

'One of our lads told the police, "We'll go quietly, but we won't go cleanly." So it's now official: we're the dirtiest team in football!'

Players are at their most vulnerable in the showers. Stephen Brasher of Perfidious Albion remembers one game at Mile End when he came out of the showers to find his clothes had been stolen. 'They'd even taken my overcoat and DMs. I had to walk home in my muddy football kit. One lad was playing his first game for us. He'd come all the way from Bedfordshire. His business suit had gone and the thieves had found his keys with a BMW emblem on them. He raced out to the car park to find his company BMW had gone too. He never played for us again.'

The scene in the showers after most games must resemble the trenches: the mud, the clogged drains, the empty shampoo bottles, the sweaty kit and discarded jockstraps. But, believe it or not, spying on a football team in the shower is apparently the stuff of sexual fantasy for some women.

In 1996, Dulwich Hamlet players starred in the video *Dream Team: A Football Fantasy* (Blue Mask, £12.99). Billed as football's answer to The Chippendales, it was enough to get any woman in a lather. The video followed Tara, a devoted female fan, who hid in the changing rooms and watched her Diadora League idols unleash their wedding tackle in the showers. It was quite literally steamy stuff from a team too sexy for their shirts. Hunky Hamlet star Russell Edwards explained: 'The lads are always dropping their trousers in the bar anyway, so no one minded doing it.'

Now, showers might be seen as sexy, but at Sunday league level news of a woman ref in the showers with the players must have risked several cardiac arrests among the gents of the Devon FA. In 1996, 41-year-old referee Janet Fewings – one of only around 400 female refs in Britain – became fed up with the women's changing rooms always being closed whenever she officiated in Exeter and District Sunday League matches. So to make a statement she started showering with the men, oblivious to the risks of any potential Norman Bates in the Exeter Sunday League. The local paper was soon reporting the mixed shower scenes, alleging complaints from jealous wives and girlfriends. (Although most Sunday league Don Juans would probably run 26 miles if confronted by a real-life naked woman in the showers.)

Fewings posed for a picture behind a shower curtain for the *Exeter Express and Echo* and argued: 'I go to a match showered. I'd love to come away showered and fresh like everybody else. I'm being victimised.'

There was no need for players' girlfriends to be jealous, she said. 'I'll share my gel, but I've one golden rule: if anyone drops the soap they leave it where it is. I can still show the red card up to fifteen minutes after the end of the match. I don't mind a bit of messing around, but I've got four kids so I've seen it all before . . . and sometimes it's not the prettiest sight in the world anyway.' The poor woman should surely have had her match fee doubled for having to witness the jellybelly stomachs of Exeter's finest pub players.

Strangely, the Devon FA did not exclaim, 'Fewings, what a scorcher!' at the sight of Janet behind the shower curtain in the national press. The committee was affronted by the steamy shower tales and charged Fewings with bringing the game into disrepute. At her hearing, Fewings refused to sign an undertaking not to talk to the media and was suspended. She was eventually reinstated but in January 1997 she received a letter from the local FA sending her for an early bath. She was sacked, not for showering with the lads, but according to the local FA, on the grounds of 'consistently low' assessment marks.

But, despite naked women refs, the risks of third-degree burns, hypothermia and the frequent discovery of thermal springs and glacial meltwater in the changing rooms, there isn't much that can surprise the Sunday stalwart in the showers. Or at least there wasn't until the Greyhound team in Swindon watched *The Full Monty* and performed the ultimate soccer strip. The lads were so elated by a 16-3 win over rivals Littentree in the Carlsberg Pub Cup that players Jason Holt and Kevin Roberts suggested they mark the victory with some nude labour.

The lads dispensed with showers altogether and ran naked out of the changing rooms and back on to the pitch. Luckily, it was a mild November lunchtime rather than a freezing January day, otherwise it might have been more a case of Dustin Hoffman's *Little Big Man* than *The Full Monty*. With only footballs covering their wedding tackle, the dirty players then posed for a souvenir photo in front of a stunned crowd. Never could the playing fields of Swindon have seen so much wobbly flesh or white skin.

Martin Goodfellow, landlord of the Greyhound, approved of the side's naked aggression. 'The lads thought they'd gone the full Monty on the pitch so they should go the full Monty off it as well. It was hysterical; no one knew which way to look. It helped that they're all the same shape as the chaps in the film.' Which was, well, imperfect.

For years the authorities have been attempting to clean up the game, but without success. All attempts at reform have remained as sporadic as the trickle from a suspect nozzle, and dirty players can still be found in public bars throughout the land. Footballers – they're a right shower.

12 Money's Too Tight to Mention

Gareth Southgate is standing with his arms folded by the Aston Villa dressing-room door.

'Bloody Stan "No Mates" Collymore has sneaked off early again without paying his subs! Just 'cos he's been substituted he's gone off in his new motor. And if he is here it's always, "I'm changing American Express cards" or, "I'm saving up to buy my mum a present."'

'Now come on, lads – £55 each. Fair's fair, eh? No, Dwight, I haven't got change for a £100 note! Oi! Bosnich! Stop doing that funny walk and pay up! And Mark Draper, don't run off once you've been interviewed by John Motson. Do us a favour and ask Ugo Ehiogu for his subs, will you? He's a big bloke and I don't want to upset him. I'll let him threaten you first.'

It's just as well that professional footballers don't have to pay weekly subs otherwise conversations like this might be occurring in every dressing room. But, unlike the pros, Sunday footballers pay – or at least should do – for the privilege of playing the sport they love. Most clubs depend on weekly payments to cover referees' fees, league administration charges and pitch payments. Not that any sense of social justice pervades most sweaty players eager to get to the bar. Generally, the Sunday league footballer likes to play it tight.

Collecting the subs is the job any secretary of any Sunday football club dreads. It might only be £1.50 or £2 a week, but footballers and their small change are not easily prised apart.

If they can find a way of not paying, they will. One common technique for the player with short arms and long pockets is to volunteer to be subbed. Could his groin strain be playing up? Is this an altruistic gesture to give the twelfth man a run out? No on both counts: it's simply a way of ensuring he's changed and out of the dressing room before the subs are collected. Other players are showered and away in minutes, while the harassed secretary is still negotiating payment details with the ref. 'I've paid you already' is a much-used technique, while lack of change seems to be an endemic problem among footballers.

Being a secretary requires more negotiating skills than Henry Kissinger, David Owen or Mo Mowlam. In 1995, Ron Hailey, the newly appointed secretary of St Augustine's in Dagenham, Essex, bemoaned his thankless task in a letter to *FC* magazine: 'Virtually all the problems seem to be caused by the players: late signing of registration forms, late payment of subs, not completing the paperwork properly, not reading circulated club papers – and then asking all sorts of questions to which they should know the answer. I was told when I agreed to do the job that I should treat everybody as children – players, opposition managers, league management committees, etc. I thought it was meant to be a joke, but no. I bet Paul Ince, Roy Keane and Ryan Giggs don't forget to give their kit back to be washed or lose their registration forms down the back of the sofa.'

Darren Murphy of the Ship Inn in Wirral says his manager has a special technique for ensuring payment. 'He stands by the dressing-room door so that no one can leave without passing him.'

Matthew Coulbeck of London side A3 Milan has another tip: 'We collect the subs before the game, as the players tend to scuttle off afterwards.' But even that tactic doesn't always work. 'We had one player who was like royalty; he never carried money,' says Coulbeck. 'He was actually quite rich; so well off that he didn't see the importance of paying subs. He owed £40 subs and then managed to walk out of our £25-a-head annual dinner without paying!'

Some teams, like London's All Nations' Club, offered a discounted rate for the unemployed and students – a welfare system that is open to abuse. 'You get people who say they are students and can't afford it, and then you realise they've driven off in a Ford Sierra chatting on a mobile phone,' moans former player-manager Gareth Smyth, who was so tired of collecting the subs that he took a job in Beirut. Maybe such teams should introduce means-tested concessions.

'We drive our own cars to away matches, and the same two or three always say, "But I need the money for petrol,"' complains Mark Edwards of Hereford side Hearts FC. 'I've also had players ask, "Can you change a £50 note?" They know that if you've just paid the ref then you'll be short of change. And there are the usual excuses like, "I haven't been to the cashpoint yet", "I'm a bit short this week" and "I haven't been paid yet". Then when you chase them up the following week they say, "But I thought I paid you."'

And imagine trying to get money out of a team of Yorkshiremen. 'They're just tight. You wouldn't believe how difficult it is getting £2 out of them,' says David Preston, secretary of the Green Man in Dewsbury, West Yorkshire. 'We get everything from, "My wife won't give me any money" to, "I'm taking my girlfriend out for dinner." And there's always "Can you change a £20 note?" You tell them you *have* got change and the excuses change!'

Green Man manager Martin Brook adopts the direct approach if arrears continue burgeoning: 'I confront them and tell them, "You'd better pay up or I'll set the big lads on you." It usually works.'

Most teams eventually resort to a no pay/no play policy. But it can be more difficult if the debtor is the Stan Bowles of the Sunday league. 'We had one player who owed £60,' says Denis Wilson of Essex side Harold Wood Hospital FC. 'He never had any money but if he did pay you'd see him in the betting shop trying to win back his subs. He couldn't afford £1.50 a game, but he could afford a three-way yankee! We had to throw him out, but it was a shame because he was our top scorer.' Wilson has had trouble with other players too: 'They say, "I'll pay you next week" – and then you see them buying a round in the pub.'

Perhaps incentives are the answer. The Windy Millers in Nuneaton encouraged their players to buy their tasteful new tartan kit a couple of seasons ago through a kind of HP scheme. After a player paid for his deluxe outfit, he paid reduced subs of £1 per game. Another solution for the more affluent club is to introduce standing orders from players' bank accounts. And no doubt players will be paying by Internet in a few years' time.

John Stannard of New Corinthians in the Linley Haulage Sunday League in Hull has had to put up with feeble excuses like, 'My dog ate my wallet.' Other legendary dog-eared excuses from the New Corinthians have included, 'I spent it all last night on my night out,' 'I paid you last week, I'm sure I did!' and 'I lost my money on the way to the match.' And there's always, 'As I'm sub again I don't deserve to have to pay subs' and, 'I'll pay if you lend me a quid.'

Phil Colver of Birmingham's Colinthians recalls one particularly devious technique. 'One of the most blatant dodges I can remember is a player going home after the game in full sweaty kit. Before the game started he'd promised to pay me but he never returned to the changing room after the game.' Clearly grime does pay. 'Another novel excuse I've had is, "I'm in the process of changing banks but there's been a delay and I still don't have a new cheque book," ' complains Colver.

Colver also identifies the 'circular' blag, where three or more players bamboozle the harassed secretary by using more verbal evasions and sophistry than any civil servant being 'economic with the truth' could manage:

Dave: 'Pete's got mine. He'll be here in a bit.'

Pete: 'John's paying for me. He owes me a tenner.'

John: 'Roy's paying mine. I paid his last week.'

Maybe honesty is best. Colver reflects: 'If they just say, "I can't pay this week. I'm out of work and short of cash," they'll win respect for being a genuine sportsman.'

However, if desperate, your side could always try a touch of Margaret Thatcher-style 'handbagging'. The Sun in Reading engaged the manager's girlfriend to collect the subs. 'She was like Hitler and no one dared not pay,' says an insider. The Iron Lady of Reading completely terrified the hapless players.

'She works for a bank, so she's used to hearing pathetic excuses about money. She'd sit in the pub after the game, her eyes glazing over, and just shout "Subs!" If they didn't have it she'd shout, "You can pay bloody double next week!" Then she'd phone them up all the time and hassle them until they paid up out of exasperation. My God, she knew how to collect a debt.'

As the Daleks used to say on *Doctor Who*: resistance is futile. Recalcitrant players should pay up now – and yes, the secretary does have change for a £50 note.

HOW TO AVOID BEING SUBBED: THE TOP EXCUSES

Can you change a £20 note?

The dog ate my wallet

I thought I'd already paid you

My wallet's in my other trousers

My wife won't give me any money

There's no money in the cashpoint

I've got to take my girlfriend out to dinner

I need the money for petrol

I forgot I was playing today

I'm just going to nip back home to get it

I'll pay you in the pub

I've left the money in the car

My bill for installing satellite TV just arrived

I haven't been paid yet

I'm a bit short this week

I'll pay you next week

I haven't been to the cashpoint yet

The CSA has been on to me

I'm still paying off my fine for GBH

13 The XXXX-Files

'Hey, Scully, take a look at this. They look like helicopter tracks.'

'On a Sunday league pitch – in the Scilly Isles? There has to be some rational scientific explanation for this, Mulder.'

'This is bigger than that, Scully. Did you ever read "A Ringer's paper on the paranormal and psychic energy present in the vicinity of the near-post header on pitch 63 at Hackney Marshes"? Remember, this is Sunday league football we're talking about.'

Special Agents Mulder and Scully could compile their biggest ever X-File on the paranormal world of the Sunday leagues. Even Dana Scully in her lab coat and plastic gloves would struggle to explain the muddy mysteries – that is, if she wasn't mistaken for the strippagram ordered to celebrate the hungover centre-half's birthday.

There aren't many sports that could result in a helicopter on the pitch, an artificial arm hanging from the crossbar or a player being swallowed up by the pitch. As the great Bard might well have said: 'There are more things in the Linley Haulage League than are dreamt of in your philosophy.'

To Hull and back

When compared to the FA Carling Premiership, the Sunday leagues are like one of those anti-matter universes where everything is familiar, but slightly different. Bungs consist of a couple of pints in the pub. There is transfer activity, but the record fee is probably the £2 paid by Persimmon Homes

Beckett League side Kirkbymoorside to neighbours Kirkdale
United for the then 21-year-old Steve Robertshaw in 1995. And
remember, this was in north Yorkshire, where no club spends
its money lightly. The move took several days to negotiate and
caused much acrimony at Steve's old club, which was managed
by his best friend. 'The £2 was to cover registration costs, but
I've taken a lot of stick about it being a record transfer,' said
the reluctant Alan Shearer of the Persimmon Homes Beckett
League at the time of his record-breaking move.

Which is not to say that amateur clubs lack ambition. To this
day, Jurgen Klinsmann must regret missing the chance to play
in the twelfth division of the Linley Haulage Sunday League in
Hull. In 1994, the Bransholme-based side Skippers faxed a bid
to Tottenham for the ace German striker. Skippers admitted
they would have trouble matching the £2.5 million fee that
Spurs paid, but offered to pay for the striker by doing £2.5
million worth of odd jobs around the club. The Skippers players
were prepared to mow the White Hart Lane pitch, paint the
stadium, give the Spurs stars haircuts (which would surely have
been Ian Walker's only chance of a decent barnet) and babysit
for the players' children.

Skippers' Ian Holmes explained: 'On the Bransholme Estate
we have a system of bartering as some people just don't have
the money to pay directly for services. So we thought we'd
apply this system to sign Klinsmann.' Sadly, Spurs chairman
Alan Sugar, normally the most far-sighted of businessmen, did
not see the potential of bartering with the Linley Haulage cup
holders. 'I reckon Spurs were simply overawed by the bid,'
added a rueful Holmes after the deal fell through. When
Klinsmann returned to English football in 1998, it was
rumoured he was hoping to be signed by Skippers, but having
been snubbed once, the club refused to bid again and Jurgen
had to accept a return to Tottenham.

Of course, the Sunday leagues are not exactly like *The X-
Files*, where mutant prehistoric insects cocoon lumberjacks or
warring cockroaches threaten humanity, but they do have
mutant maggots in Chesterfield. Even Mulder would find it
difficult to credit that the Hasland Shoulder of Mutton FC hold

maggot-racing contests in their pub. 'We have an annual maggot-racing evening, and it's a really popular fund-raising event,' enthuses secretary Melvyn McMahon. 'Our goalkeeper has a board with lights on it and we open a book for the fastest maggot. The rest of the pub enjoys the fun of it all – but it can take a long time to get a result.' Let's hope they never get in the Bombay mix, lads.

There are even shape shifters, although it is doubtful if Alex Ferguson will be following the example of the London Fire Brigade. 'We have a pair of glasses with a penis on them,' explains the aptly named Paul Cutting, 'and we award them to the worst player on the previous Saturday. They're called the "What The Fuck Was I Doing On Saturday Glasses" and the winner has to wear them for the full hour-and-a-half training session.'

Nothing goes quite to plan in Sunday football and each game is full of tales of the unexplained. Take the Milldean forward who had persevered against disability and established a place in the side despite the handicap of only having one arm. No doubt he viewed himself as a non-league Gary Mabbutt, who's been a marvellous example to those with diabetes, acting as an ambassador for the limbless in sport. That was until he went out on to the pitch one freezing morning in south London. 'He always left his arm until last and one of the lads had hung his wooden arm up on the crossbar,' chuckles secretary George Ward. 'He wasn't too happy about it, I can tell you. But it was all a bit of armless fun really.'

Mind you football can cure disabilities remarkably quickly. Derek Russell of the Three Tuns in Hull recalls playing in a village outside Hull. 'At a lot of these village games the whole population turns out. There was this kid in the crowd who was injured on crutches. The game got a bit heated and he started threatening us. Eventually, and to our total amazement, he threw down his crutches and came on the pitch wanting to have a go at us. Then he slipped on a cow pat and fell over.'

Another cure that Jesus would have been proud of took place at a Millbank game in London. 'Oscar was our club secretary who also did the match reports and he was a bit of an eccentric,' recalls Mike Pattenden. 'He'd been injured and he was on the touchline in his windcheater, slacks and Clark's Commandos, when with ten minutes to go he decided to give his injured leg a run out. He just cast his stick aside, pulled a shirt on, and ran down the wing in his slacks and shoes. It was quite shaming really. The incident precipitated a split between those who were serious and the nellies.'

If it's not artificial arms on the crossbar, it's manholes on the pitch. Managers attempting to stop Ryan Giggs in the Premiership have never, as yet, resorted to the manhole-to-man marking tactics of south London side Lokomotiv. When the club played at the Croydon recreation ground, its secret weapon was a manhole lurking just inside the pitch. 'I knew exactly where it was,' remembers Lokomotiv's Brian Benson, 'but the number of wingers who went sliding over it was unbelievable. That manhole became like a twelfth man for us.'

Then there was the player who attempted to imitate Fabrizio Ravanelli's famous shirt-over-head goal-scoring celebration. Seventy minutes into a tense semi-final with local rivals Easington, Nick Kirk scored from the penalty spot to place Hull side Saltshouse Tavern into an unassailable 2-0 lead. Throughout Saltshouse's cup run Nick had been celebrating his goals with his Ravanelli pastiche. His team-mates were so used to the routine that they were meekly pacing back to the centre circle. Only the shirt-over-head show turned out to be more Elephant Man than Ravanelli.

'I went off on my lap of honour with my shirt pulled up. I thought I'd top it off with a somersault – but I lost my footing and collapsed in a heap. I heard a crack and I knew that it was something serious but I was too embarrassed to say anything,' remembers Kirk. He was substituted five minutes later and found to have a broken collarbone. 'Next time, I'll celebrate sensibly like Alan Shearer,' mused the prone civil servant.

Game over man

But at least nutty Nick Kirk's match was completed. A match between Peartree Sports and AFC Bitterne in the Southampton Sunday Football League was postponed for a particularly bizarre reason. After 43 minutes, a police constable walked on to the pitch to announce that an unexploded bomb had been discovered in the adjoining car park and ordered the referee to abandon the match. This was a bit of a result for Peartree, who were 5-0 down at the time, but less so for the AFC Bitterne forward who'd scored all five of his side's goals. Even worse for the forward who'd been looking forward to scoring at least ten, the bomb proved to be just a railway plating tool. In the replay, Peartree only lost 3-2 and almost inevitably, the five-goal forward didn't score once.

Games have also been stopped after the mysterious landing of unidentified flying objects. George Ward of Milldean remembers one particularly close encounter: 'In one game this model aeroplane came down on the pitch. It could have killed us. The bloke came over to pick it up and we nearly gave him a kicking!'

Collapsing goals are always a risk too. A London Spartan League Premier Division match between Hanwell Town and Brook House was postponed after a Brook House player launched himself at a cross, missed the ball and ran into the net. This sudden pressure caused the post to break off at ground level. 'We had another post to replace it, but, as it had been raining, the ground was swollen and we couldn't get the stump out,' explained Hanwell secretary John Wake. All 22 players had to troop off the field, feeling truly stumped.

On the Scilly Isles, a game between Tresco and a neighbouring St Mary's side was abandoned when a chopper landed on the pitch blowing down the goals made from paddles and fishing nets – which wasn't that surprising really as the pitch was also the island's helicopter landing strip. Another game on the Scilly Isles, against a birdwatchers XI, had to be abandoned when the twitchers heard that a yellow-bellied sapsucker had been spotted on another island. The entire team ran off the pitch in the middle of the game to go and look for it. (Which brings a whole new meaning to Frank Worthington's quote, 'My bed wasn't for sleeping, it was for birding. I was at it five nights a week.')

At the Windy Millers in Nuneaton, older players can still

recall the game where a police helicopter was swooping overhead in pursuit of an escaped prisoner playing in a Sunday league match. (Presumably, he was given a conditional discharge after the judge decided he'd suffered enough.)

And you can't imagine Peter Schmeichel and his Manchester United team-mates meekly walking off the pitch because the ref's wife has forgotten her house keys. At the end of the 1996–97 season, Northleach Town were drawing a Friday night Cheltenham League match 1-1, with six minutes remaining. It was a tense game with both sides pressing for a winner. The result was vital as Northleach needed a point to stay up. Only, suddenly, Northleach's relegation fight was interrupted by a woman pitch invader who rushed across the turf and headed straight for the referee.

'The players were going, "Who's this fucking woman?" She'd run right across the field,' sighs referee Phil Pawsey. He knew exactly who it was though. It was his wife who'd lost her house keys and needed Phil's because she was going to the theatre. And if that wasn't embarrassing enough for the ref, by the time the handover was complete, the light had faded and Pawsey was forced to abandon the game, causing great annoyance among both teams. 'Northleach were none too pleased,' admitted Pawsey. 'They lodged a complaint with the league. I offered to referee the re-match, but I never heard anything.' Luckily Northleach won the replayed 'key fixture' 4-0.

Just like in *The X-Files*, normally mild-mannered men can mysteriously turn into serial player-abusers. There have long been rumours about the Men In Black, but no one could have predicted the strange bout of kinetic energy which resulted in two players being injured by an assault with a linesman's flag. The truth was out there in Leicester Crown Court.

Neil Bassford, the assistant manager of Birstall United Old Boys, had agreed to run the line in the match against Ratby sports club.

The teams were drawing 3-3 in a cracking game of football. But, in the 89th minute, linesman Bassford thought he heard the Birstall centre forward being abused by two Ratby players. Rather than drawing the referee's attention to the incident,

38-year-old Bassford raced on to the pitch and set about two Ratby players, Ian Smith and Bret North. The crazed linesman shoved North to the ground, dislocating his shoulder, and then proceeded to clobber both players around the head with his flag, resulting in them needing three stitches each. In one of those wonderful examples of legal understatement, Bassford's defence lawyer said that the irascible linesman 'now accepted that he had gone beyond reasonable force'.

Bassford, who has now retired from football, received a two-month suspended jail sentence and was told to pay each victim £250. Judge Richard Benson commented with cutting irony: 'We all know it's a contact sport but generally speaking the players expect the contact to be between them.'

Other confrontations between Sunday league players and authority might have been less violent, but have led to some remarkable rulings. Would Ian Wright or Julian Dicks ever have approached Lancaster Gate with a dictionary, prepared to argue over the definition of the word 'bollocks'? Nick Loughlin of the White House pub side in Hartlepool was not afraid to bring in semantics when confronted by the threat of a three-week suspension for swearing at a referee. He used a dictionary to back his case that 'bollocks' was not a swear word but 'an expression of disbelief'. And it worked, too. The Durham FA took the Sex Pistols' advice to never mind the bollocks and reduced his suspension from three weeks to two.

Phone win

All good FBI agents like Mulder and Scully need their mobile phones, and the Sunday leagues are no different. In fact, the advent of the mobile surely deserves an addendum in the FA rules of the game. It might be good to talk but most referees don't think so. Tony Owen, a substitute for the Printer's Devil, was running the line in a match against AFC '79. With his side 1-0 down, Tony received a call on his mobile from manager Carl Quinlan, whose car had broken down on the M4. The boss ordered a substitution and change of formation, which Owen relayed to the lads on the pitch. While still acting as linesman, he then gave the manager a commentary on the game. At which point the referee rushed over and asked Owen what he was doing. 'I told him I was taking tips from the manager and his face turned red. He said I wasn't doing the job properly and booked me.'

The ref threatened to send him off if he used the phone again – at which point Bob Hoskins would presumably have announced, 'It's good to walk.' At least the new mobile formation worked, and the Printer's Devil ran home 3-1 winners. Manager Carl Quinlan was delighted: 'I was so happy that I almost offered to pay Tony's £10 fine for getting booked.'

Bruce Grobbelaar might have floored a penalty taker with his jelly legs in a European Cup Final, but sometimes a simple call on the mobile will suffice. Alan Bond of Newport Civil Service FC was preparing to face a penalty. The ball was on the spot, keeper and taker totally focused, when from the back of the goal Bond's phone rang. He walked to the back of the net and had a conversation with his babysitter before returning to his goal and saving the penalty.

'I always carry the mobile with me. I put it in the back of the net with my gloves and forgot about it,' explained Bond. The ref was not impressed by the call, though, booking Alan for ungentlemanly conduct. Club secretary Paul Malloy also threatened disciplinary action: 'We might confiscate his phone on match days. Everyone saw the funny side except the ref.' Alas, the match didn't end in a phone win. Bond's side lost 1-0.

Perhaps the ultimate phone goal was scored by goalkeeper Mark Sergeant, who, in November 1996, let the opposition score while he was taking a call on his mobile. The dozy custodian of Bass House in Spalding, Lincolnshire, was on the dog and bone to his girlfriend Ann, thinking that the play was safely at the other end of the pitch. She'd phoned up wanting to know why he hadn't called her earlier, as he'd promised.

Ann was saying she wanted him to pick her up after the match when suddenly Mark noticed the play moving towards his goal and began pleading with her to hang up. 'I was just telling her I had to go when the shot came in. I used the hand with the phone in to make a save but I could only push the ball out,' recalled Mark. The opposing striker blasted the rebound into the net to equalise and both sets of players ended up laughing at the hapless phone arranger.

Sergeant always takes his mobile to games and once had to tell a mate to hang on while he took a goal kick. Thankfully it didn't cost Bass House the match. 'We told him he was a right plonker but in the end we scored five minutes from time and beat Aztec Rangers 2-1, so we had a laugh about it,' says team-mate Jason Wells.

The old Stoke manager Alan Durban once said: 'If you want entertainment then go to the circus.' But then he'd never seen Murton Village Inn play. John Collings takes up the story: 'We'd had a charity fancy dress the night before and the next morning outside the dressing room we had Hitler, Noddy, the front end of a cow and a pantomime policeman. The pantomime policeman didn't get a game, but ten minutes into the match he ran on to the pitch and attacked an opposition player with his rubber truncheon. We were in stitches, although the ref wasn't too amused.' An urgent FA Commission of Inquiry into the use of rubber truncheons at football matches is expected to reach a verdict in 2010.

And what possible explanation could there be for a pitch that swallows dogs? Portsmouth is not noted for the paranormal – apart from Pompey winning the odd home game – but the match between the Three Crowns and Scotts Bar threw up an incident that will surely be filmed in B-movie style as *The Pitch That Ate Pebbles*.

The game at the King George V playing fields was only twelve minutes old when a gaping hole appeared in the Three Crowns defence – literally. When the Three Crowns' Paul Bailey went for a loose ball, a rusty manhole cover collapsed beneath him. Feeling the ground disappearing beneath him as if he'd been felled by Vinny Jones, the hapless defender managed to scramble out of the chasm that had opened up. Which surely brings a new meaning to playing in the hole.

The referee stopped the game, but it was too late to prevent the Three Crowns' inquisitive mascot, a Yorkshire Terrier called Pebbles, from racing on to the pitch and plunging ten feet down the hole into a pool of muddy water. In a scene that will surely be re-enacted on 999, the non-swimming dog was now in danger of drowning. It was a hole new ball game, but, thankfully, linesman John Guinelly valiantly attempted to rescue the floundering mutt by fearlessly flinging himself into the fissure. 'As I was hanging on to a few metal hooks in the manhole I just managed to grab her by the neck and pull her up. Pebbles was shaking like a leaf when we got her out,' explains the brave lino. What other sport could combine disaster, heroism, earthquakes, floods and being kind to animals?

The Three Crowns lost the replayed game 2-0, prompting goalkeeper Gary Collis to comment, 'We've had a few injuries. Maybe half the team has been swallowed by manholes.'

Sunday league football – even Chris Carter couldn't script it.

14 The Lad Done Bard

If nothing else, Sunday football is good for the literary arts. Seemingly every club has a resident wit who produces a weekly programme, match report or news sheet. New technology has made the task easier. Numerous illicitly used firm photocopiers and word processors, and increasing numbers of home PCs are used to update details of the lads' performances, both in the pub and on the pitch. Sunday league literature is surely, like most of its writers' waistlines, the next big thing. And let's not forget conceptual art either – most clubs could knock out the sort of stuff seen at the RA's Sensation exhibition given several pints of beer, a few bare bums and an office photocopier.

We all like to see our names in print, and the advantage with the club mag is that everyone recognises the in-jokes. And the fact that they're repeated week after week somehow makes them funnier. Desmond Morris, author of *The Soccer Tribe*, once wrote that if you opened any address book it would have around 100 names in it, which is roughly the number in a pre-industrial tribal settlement. Running the club fanzine allows certain individuals to impress and entertain their peer group, the players, their girlfriends, families and children, while satisfying the competitive urge among naked apes to gain tribal status.

Some writers will go to unusual lengths to stimulate their readers. In Reading, the editor of the Sun's newsletter 'The Referee's a Wanker' is a man who uses the pseudonym of Allan Shaftbottom (it's presumably best not to ask how he got it). He once made an extraordinary offer to the club's top scorer. Referring to the club's 'new, rather foul-mouthed enthusiastic supporter, whose name shall not be mentioned (clue: she's got lovely jugs – Ed)', Shaftbottom went on to allege that, 'One player Matty "Hello Sailor" Jones received a leg rub and a soapy tit wank prior to his triumphant goal-scoring appearance against the Misfits and doctors say that he will never be the same again.' He then offered the same treatment to whoever finished as the club's top goal-scorer at the end of the season. The soap expert in question was Shaftbottom's wife. Sadly, she declined to perform the said services at the awards ceremony.

A win can be so much more satisfying when immortalised in print and Steve Wright (aka Wrightiniho) of Brazil 70 knows how to celebrate a victory in the club's weekly fanzine *Brazil Nuts*. The club's first-ever victory was greeted by the banner headline 'Bloody Brazilliant!' and the assertion that in future years people will ask, in the manner of President Kennedy's assassination, 'Where were you when Brazil 70 beat Rivets Reserves?' A 4-0 win over Chiltern Railways was greeted by the pun-laden 'Railwaymen Show The Strain As Brazil Stay On Track' while a valiant 3-1 triumph over Allied Westman earnt the euphoric 'Dance Dance Wherever You May Be, The Brilliant Boys From Brazil Score Three!!!' Even a 9-0 defeat by International Young Boys was greeted with an almost upbeat headline of 'Brazil Whipped by Young Boys!!'

A standard way of getting everyone involved in the club spirit is the player profile. This is a parody of the sort of thing you used to find in *Shoot*, only usually ten times more obscene. The Windy Millers in Nuneaton produced an, ahem, in-depth profile of an intense player nicknamed Captain Deep. It went like this:

Favourite group: Deep Purple, Depeche Mode.
Favourite Song: 'Down Down Deeper And Down' by Status Quo, 'Going Underground' by the Jam.
Miscellaneous dislikes: Living with moles, happy people, living just below hell, stripy shirts, smiling, life in general.
Miscellaneous likes: Deep-sea diving, potholing, being down, sitting in graveyards, climbing so that I can visit my mates who work at the pit.
Favourite chat-up lines: I'd like to go down on you. I want a deep relationship.

Occupation: Painting the underside of pavements.

Friends: Dick Dunn, Kenny Dalglish, Howard Hughes, the Worm family from next door.

Favourite holiday spots: Australia, Equator, Costa Del Soil.

Ambitions: To go downhill from here. To be generally sad.

Football Ambitions: To play deep midfield on a downhill slope on a bleak night in the middle of deepest darkest Africa.

And that was a player they liked. Any player who failed to pass the Windy Millers collective lunacy test was denounced in the club magazine with a zeal that wouldn't have been out of place in *Pravda*. Poor 'Mr Spoons' suffered a profile that listed all his nicknames ('Norman No-Mates, Jarhead, Captain Wobbly'), claimed his chat-up lines were, 'Hello darling, hi baby, all right love, sorry for being such a boring ugly c**t,' and described his natural skills as, 'Being a creep, being a fudgepacker, going out with old tarts, having no mates.' His ambition was listed as, 'To be asked to wear make-up when starring in *The Elephant Man*.'

Another easy way of keeping the side's interest is the form report. At the end of each match report, the players are given marks out of ten by the omnipotent editor, and a humorous or biting comment is added next to the mark. An old Milldean match programme for the London and Kent Border League match against Bromley Royals is a fine example of the genre, and had the following comments about the 6-3 reverse at Morley:

1. S. Mandry: *Still* hasn't saved a penalty. (7)

2. P. Hayes: Bring back Kenny Sansom. (6)

3. D. Hutchins: I thought he was a traffic cop. (6)

4. G. Ward: Talk about a sulk. (6)

5. D. Francis: Played like a battleship (the Bismark). (7)

6. M. Mandry: Tackled on Old Greenwich Mean Time. (6)

7. S. Spencer: Played like Mr Blobby. (6)

8. B. Pool: 100 per cent penalty record. Lucky bastard. (7)

9. K. Lockhart: Man of the match. Should have scored more goals! (8)

10. M. Potter: Ran everywhere. Got nowhere? (6)

11. L. Flockton: NO COMMENT. (−10) [He was sent off for hitting the ref.]

12. W. Collings: Played like a pitbull without the muzzle. (6)

13. L. Jerome: Like the Polaris, a good sub. (6)

A serious note after the team marks also proved that the programme is the best way of getting disciplinary points across. Referring to the previous week's sending off, the editor warned: 'The club will not tolerate the disgraceful sort of behaviour as displayed on Sunday. We will adhere strictly to any suspension dealt out by the London FA and London Kent Border League as this sort of stupidity will have grave consequences at the end of the season and may result in the club being suspended and having to apply for re-election.' The message was all the more effective for coming after the usual club humour and banter.

There are even Sunday league poets. Thanks to the efforts of the Poetry Society and funds from the National Lottery, poets are being hired by the likes of the BBC, Marks & Spencer, prisons, solicitors, canteens and gardens. Even Barnsley FC have their own poet, Ian McMillan, who presumably has stanza room only on match days. Yet many Sunday league clubs, devoid of Arts Council and National Lottery funding, had their own poets in residence years before it became fashionable. And they come without a fee.

The Windy Millers have The Gay Poet (a title which may or may not be post-modern irony) in residence, otherwise known as goalkeeper Keith T. Jones. Over the years, he's kept the lads amused with such epics as 'Cheer Up Fatty Lane':

Oh I could fly without wings
On the back of Laney's things
At quarter to eleven I'm as happy as can be
Cos Laney is so near, we'll all give a cheer
For he can't fit into our strip
Cheer up Fatty Lane
Oh what can it mean
To the rest of the team
That you're not playin'
We once thought of you as a slim bastard, that's untrue
For you're a fat bastard through and through
We all dreamt of the day
When the fat bastard would not play
And now our dreams are coming true.

Some programme editors can have a rather grandiose idea of their potential readership. Steve Hurst, a former player with the London Civil Service Third XI recalls a mad editor who would regularly produce the *Civil Service Review and Programme* (which unfortunately assumed the acronym of CRAP).

'It was better than most fanzines and became a real cult thing,' says Hurst, proudly producing his back copies of *CRAP*. These include letters from the editor Barra McGachy asking the Pope (a left-footed keeper currently playing for Vatican FC) for his blessing. He also dispatched a missive to the Prince of Wales asking him to help fund a new architecturally pleasing stand, and sent an offer of a manageress job to Cherie Lunghi (who played the title role in the TV drama *The Manageress*) as she is 'the right person to bring the glory days back to the Civil Service FC'. McGachy was aware of women's increasing involvement in Sunday league football and assured Lunghi of adequate childcare provision for her daughter. Sadly, she turned down the job, a hasty decision she must still rue.

Replies were received to all the letters, the most memorable being an affirmation that the Pope 'is praying for you and members of your football club. He invokes upon all of you God's blessings of grace and peace.' Blimey. Maybe His Holiness can play in goal if the lads are short at the weekend.

Yes, Sunday league literature is a much-neglected genre, but with greater exposure it will hopefully receive the recognition it deserves, not to mention numerous Arts Council grants. Melvyn Bragg might not realise it as yet, but footballers are men of letters – even if for most of them it's great big capital ones.

15 Who's the W**ker in the Black?

'Linesman . . . linesman, what sort of thing is happening here? What have they been instructed . . . The referee's just lost me my job . . . thank him for that, won't you . . .'

In the *Do I Not Like That* video, Graham Taylor proved that even England bosses can totally lose it. He rants at the referee in the manner of an earlier England manager, King Lear, whose side played upon a desolate stormy heath, while their boss shouted defiance at the wind and rain and thunderbolts.

So imagine what it's like reffing in the Sunday leagues where the linesmen (sorry, referee's assistants, to use their silly new name) are often subs, managers, spectators or a bloke with his dog. They are likely to be still hungover, biased towards their own side and ignorant of the rules of the game. Even worse, the more belligerent subs-turned-linesmen might attempt to insert their flags up the orifices of recalcitrant players. While for the ref, both managers can seem to be psychos and the players all resemble Iain Dowie clones. And at this level there's always the risk of interruption from herds of cows, collapsing manholes or psycho players driving their cars at you on the pitch.

Every decision is disputed. Every throw-in is argued over, the most blatant penalties are dismissed as a dive by the offending side, and no defender will ever admit that they failed to step up and played that forward onside. There are around 32,500 referees in England and every one of them is a useless cretin according to most players and spectators. Even some professional footballers can't resist the urge to query the Sunday refs' decisions. In January 1988, Leicester's Garry Parker was charged by the FA after haranguing a referee in a Sunday league match between Cherwell Lions, managed by his father-in-law Ray Timms, and local rivals Cowley Cosmos.

Parker is a supporter of the Lions and regularly runs the line for the Oxford Sunday League division four side. So for once, that bloke on the touchline shouting 'I could do better than that!' really could. And imagine the surprise of the opposition manager who says to that stroppy git on the line, 'Oi! Who do you think you are? Garry Parker?' only to be answered by, 'Yes, I am Garry Parker actually.' Still, a pint and sausage and chips in the pub afterwards must beat Martin O'Neill worrying if Leicester are safe from relegation yet.

If you're useless and you've lost then it's always a comfort to criticise the ref in the pub. After the game, the referee's parenthood, eyesight, age and sexual orientation are all questioned. And just occasionally, when the referee has hardly been noticed, the players might admit that he or she has had a good game.

There's the 85-year-old ref who never leaves the centre circle, the ref with the bottle-top glasses, or the one who's so young he looks like your son. Referees can start at sixteen and ref until they drop, so it's no wonder they vary. For example, in 1996, Dave Higgs was still reffing at the age of 71 in the Old Boys and Southern Olympian League in London. He started reffing when he was 33 and said: 'I still like refereeing and I don't think players are any worse now. To anyone just taking it up, I would say keep at it and don't let the hassle put you off. It's worth the trouble.'

'We once had a Christian ref,' says Hugh Jones of Perfidious Albion, grimacing. 'It wasn't just that he booked anyone for swearing – it was any blasphemy. He'd book you for saying "Jesus Christ!" and "Oh, bugger!" – even the mildest expletives. And believe it or not we only got him because his mother, who's a ref, wasn't available. We tried not to be outwardly hostile to him in the pub, but then he said, "I hope I did OK. I'm just preparing for my theological exams and I was trying to referee in the spirit of a Christian."'

Another bizarre stoppage involving the Albion came when a ball was stolen during a game at Haggerston Park: 'It's a rough area of London and the pitch is by a huge council estate. All the local kids hang around watching the game. When the ball was hoofed off, these local kids belted off into the estate. The ref was a big Scouser, and even though we'd got another ball he wasn't going to let a bunch of scallies nick the ball. So he gave chase and so did the players. It went on for about fifteen minutes until the kids ran into the estate pub. We all thought, Hang on, we're not going in there, and went back to the pitch. Only, we couldn't complete the match as our booking had finished.'

The typical Sunday ref is probably someone who's played until their mid-30s, but still wants to be involved in football. David Elleray and virtually every top-class referee started off in the Sunday leagues. Although many people believe that it takes years to make it to the top, the likes of Mike Riley from Leeds are only in their early 30s and officiating at Premiership matches.

At Sunday league level, the referee needs what might euphemistically be described as 'presence'. One ref at Hackney Marsh has 'LOVE' tattooed on one hand and 'HATE' on the other. Not too many players dispute his decisions.

Dave Braddish is a chirpy London geezer who knows how to give back the verbals if he gets aggro from a player called Spam Head. He is active in the Fulham and District Referees' Society and officiates with humour and common sense. He appreciates that the players are out there for a good kickabout and a drink afterwards.

'I try to use a sense of humour, and if that doesn't work I go back to what the book says,' says Braddish. 'A bloke called me a c**t once and technically I could have sent him off. But after he missed a chance I said to him quietly, "You just missed an open goal – who's the c**t?" The player and the captain both heard it and he calmed down and turned to me and said, "I get your point." It's man-management. Good refs say that Law 18 is common sense.'

Braddish is 40 and took up refereeing in the Fulham Sportsman's League in London after he was injured sixteen years ago, having once been on Chelsea's books. He is general manager of a window cradle company and is paid £15 a game plus travel expenses.

'I do it to keep involved,' says Dave. 'You're putting something back into the game which is very satisfying. I don't get too much abuse as I'm not a small fella and I tend to give it back, which helps.

'Personality is the secret of being a good ref. You don't bend the laws but you use them to your advantage. Sometimes you have players doing things off the ball. You know it's going on but you can't see it. So you get them on technicalities later and make sure they're out of the game and they haven't won.'

Potential flare-ups can be calmed through the force of Braddish's character. 'Once I booked the keeper and he said his name was Spam Head. I said, "Right, Mr Spam Head, you've got the showers to yourself now." All his team-mates cracked up laughing as they realised what an idiot he was.'

It takes an unusual combination of events to defeat the indefatigable Braddish. 'I had a Schumacher situation once where the keeper had come out and brought the forward down. An ambulance was on the pitch. Then a helicopter landed! I said, "That's enough," and postponed the game. The thing was I'd been paid before the game. That was the best result of my career!'

So what else makes a good referee? David Ager, the author of *The Soccer Referee's Manual* and a licensed instructor of referees in the Cornwall area agrees that just knowing the law isn't enough. 'It's a bit like understanding the highway code. You can know all the traffic laws, understand the braking distances, but it doesn't mean you can drive.

'During the referees' courses we do role playing on how to handle things like booking a player. During a game there's lots of adrenaline flowing and it's extremely easy to inflame the situation.

'The basic rule is to remain firm and in control, but show the player respect. Don't bawl him out, wave your arms around, order him around, touch him or lecture him. You do it formally and say, "I'm cautioning you for ungentlemanly conduct. If you repeat the offence you may be sent off." A moral lecture is always a bit disastrous.

'When I ref I try to explain things. Players are often genuinely unsure why you've made a decision. They say, "What's that for?" If you say, "Indirect free kick for dangerous play," they respect you for explaining.'

Peter Willis of the Referees' Association suggests that you've got to have a love of the game and a basic level of fitness. 'And you've got to remember that although your ability as a ref might not be exceptional, the teams in Sunday leagues aren't that good either, even though they all think they should be playing for Arsenal. Much of it is about man-management. There are only seventeen laws of the game and they're not too difficult to learn.'

'The problem with many referees today is that they don't talk to players; they talk down to them rather than to them. And they're too quick to get cards out,' says Alex Myers, a former referee who now runs and provides referees for several local leagues and is a London FA councillor. Like Braddish, he prefers the humorous approach.

'I used to say, "Be careful. I'm a magician. I can make you vanish any time," or if I saw a couple arguing in the penalty area I'd call them over and say, "Is there any chance of coming to the wedding, because the way you two are going on, I assume you're getting married." Another one was when players were giving me backchat. I'd say, "There's two refs here and I'm getting paid. What are you doing?" It made them think. If you talk down to them it puts their back up in a situation you could have killed stone dead with a bit of good refereeing.'

But imagine the stick you get from players for being both a woman ref and in the police force. Just as Wendy Toms became the first woman linesman in Football League history in 1994, so the Sunday leagues have their pioneering women refs bravely entering the world of sweaty jockstraps and macho expletives. South London referee Georgina Christoforou had to take the South-East Counties League to the Equal Opportunities Commission to become an official. She used to play and thought she could ref better than some of the refs she'd seen.

'As I'm in the police force I'm used to dealing with difficult people,' says Georgina. 'If you lay the law down early you don't get much abuse. In a way, it's easier for me to keep control of

men. They don't swear as much and sometimes if one player
swears his team-mates tell him not to. They'll try things on with
throw-ins and make a few sexist comments about joining them
in the showers. I normally say, "I may be fed up but I'm not
hard up." But as soon as they step over the mark they're
booked.

'You get a good rapport with the players. I was miked up for
a TV documentary once and all the players made a point of
swearing as they ran past and saying, "She only does it to be
on the telly." It was really funny.'

From a referee's perspective, some Sunday league players and
managers can make Coventry's Gordon Strachan seem like a ref
lover. Faced with one insult too far, Janet Walmsley, a
long-serving London referee, once fulfilled the ultimate fantasy
of every man or woman in black.

'I've walked off at Mile End,' says Janet, who as a woman
ref in the male world of the Sunday leagues has learnt to take
no abuse from anyone. When she started reffing in the early
1980s, she would arrive at games on her 250cc motorbike.
'They didn't quite know what to expect, but I find the new
generation of footballers are more used to working with women
and having a woman in charge of them.'

Her Mile End walkout occurred during a match in a business
league: 'Some guy had decided that he wanted to be the ref and
was disputing every decision. Then he said, "I don't think we
need a ref." So I said, "Right, if he can't keep his big mouth
shut I'm walking off. I don't need this aggro. I'm going!" Then
they were all pleading with me to come back. But when they
try to take control, that's it. I'm the sort of person who will just
go.' Walmsley left the pitch and the players were left like
naughty children to reflect that without referees there could be
no football. Such walkouts are rare, however, and Walmsley
now has the ultimate referee on her side – God. The Good Lord
himself would surely have been tempted to show the red card
to some pub defenders in the Judean Sunday League games, so
we shouldn't be surprised that referees need spiritual help.

Perhaps reflecting that if Jesus laid on the cross, most of the
players she was in charge of couldn't head it in, Walmsley

rediscovered her Christian faith, attending church on Sunday evenings after a hard morning's reffing and blinding. 'I do pray at half-time for the players and it does help me to keep calm,' says Walmsley. 'You feel the presence of the Lord on the pitch and I think my prayers have saved me from a lot of difficult situations.' Yes, Sunday league footballers really are a bunch of miserable sinners.

Sadly, as in any sport, enthusiasm and competitiveness can spill over into violence, but, despite the frequent tabloid accounts of assaults on referees, these cases are still, thankfully, relatively rare. Most referees could go through a career without mishap says David Ager: 'I did a little statistical exercise with the number of referees and assaults and I calculated that on average you'd be assaulted once in 40 years, which isn't too bad.'

Peter Willis agrees: 'You have to remember that there are something like 90,000 games or more every weekend. There are about 350 assaults a season and you can count the number of serious assaults on one hand. But you have to be able to recognise that glint in the eye. A quick card from ten yards can stop an incident but sometimes it's better to take them aside and have a word.'

But, although the danger of on-pitch violence might have been exaggerated by the media, when such incidents do occur they can be gloriously bizarre. In 1994, a game in Nottingham was abandoned after the ref was chased by an irate player driving a van. Referee Wayne Kirkham had sent off an Old Rose player in the Notts Combination League match between Old Rose and Hucknall Chequers. In what must have resembled the final scene of the film *The Cars That Ate Paris* crossed with *Wacky Races*, the aggrieved Old Rose player clambered into his van and drove it on to the pitch and straight at the referee. Kirkham had to run away from the van's path and was then shielded by Chequers players. This early example of road rage merged with ref rage resulted in the van driver being charged with grievous bodily harm.

The ultimate referee's nightmare was experienced by 53-year-old Terry Pattinson. In 1995, he was involved in one of the strangest stoppages in the history of football, while reffing a game in the Chiswick and District League between two 'enthusiastic' pub sides. One player had not only that glint in his eye, but a glint on the blade of his sword too.

Early in the game there was an initial fight between two players off the ball. One of the other players told the ref that the argument had started because 'one of our lads asked him for a kiss'. As trouble simmered, one of the managers, with his side 0-3 down, made the brave decision to substitute the non-kissing player. At half-time Pattinson congratulated the pub gaffer on his common-sense management of a tense situation.

But it wasn't the last of the substituted player. His side were 4-0 down after 60 minutes and he had returned to the touchline in jeans and a bomber jacket. Pattinson was looking at a goalmouth mêlée when one of the players suggested that he take a look at what was happening at the other end of the pitch. The substituted player had returned, only now he was grappling with one of his own players. The players watched the fight, but when the subbed player began to fear a points decision going against him, he drew a sword from his jacket. Presumably he now wanted a role as a buccaneering midfielder.

Most of the players scarpered. We can only pity the poor ref, suddenly confronted with what must have looked like an extra from *The Three Musketeers* rampaging across the pitch. Then the swordsman stabbed one of his players in the thigh and blood spattered over the pitch.

Faced with this bladerunner, Pattinson had little choice but to abandon the match even though it was presumably balanced on a knife edge. Proving conclusively that football is not more important than life and death, the beleaguered ref announced, 'I'm not prepared to die for the sake of football.' He later explained to a spectator, with commendable understatement, that 'I was very concerned that hostile swordplay would have a bad effect in the middle of a match.'

The rampaging and quite possibly deranged swordsman was eventually overpowered beneath a scrum of team-mates and led off the pitch. That would have been enough for most players, but there's always one who carries on complaining.

'You can't abandon it – we're 4-0 up,' moaned a player from the winning side.

'Look at it this way. What would you say if you got run through the chest when your mind was only on taking a corner kick?' countered Pattinson.

Rumours that the subbed player later had trials with Sheffield United, nicknamed the Blades, could not be substantiated, although the errant swordsman would surely have appealed to Wimbledon with his ability to run through defences. But, thanks to his intervention, we have been left one of the most surreal referee's reports in footballing history. It ended with the matter-of-fact, 'Match abandoned in 60th minute due to intervention of knife maniac.'

But, despite the risk of abuse or occasional assault by rampaging swordsmen, the men in black are usually up for anything. But even the best refs sometimes baulk at certain matches.

'There are two unofficial rules among referees,' laughs David Ager. 'The first is don't ref games between policemen. Disciplined and controlled as they may be on the street, on the pitch they're bloody lethal.'

Honest, ref, he just fell down the stairs . . . Ager continues to reminisce about the Old Bill at play: 'I'll always remember one police game I reffed where one side only had nine players. A carful of officers had got lost. I was almost tempted to suggest that they ask a policeman for the way, but their manager was a big bloke.

'The second rule is don't ever handle matches between referees – they're absolutely murderous, as every single decision is disputed and dissected.'

They are the men and women in black. They've been among us for years. And now they've established such a large colony in earthbound footballing society that we can't live without their advanced alien technology of a pea and whistle.

16 A Life of Two Halves

Five female footie fans are lined up on the balcony of the Flying Pig clubhouse. They're playing with baby Jack Cousins, son of club secretary Joanne Griffiths and goalkeeper Stewart Cousins, watching the game but also animatedly discussing a big night out at Chicago's bar and the nuances of various friends' love lives.

Women Sunday league watchers generally fall into three categories. There are those who are in the first flush of love and turn up every week to watch their hot date, those who genuinely enjoy the game, and football widows who are hoisted out of bed to watch the game but then spend 90 minutes reading a book. Perhaps the record for partner apathy is held by Hugh Jones of Perfidious Albion. 'Lynne came along to watch me play and within 90 seconds she'd left to go for a walk in Mile End Park, which is a pretty horrible urban park at the best of times. It was the one time she'd watched me and we soon reverted to normal form and lost 8-0, so I suffered a lot of ridicule about that.'

But here at the Flying Pig there is a mix of football lovers and haters. Club secretary Joanne Griffiths is a fan of the game. She has definitely seen an increase in female interest at the club. 'I knew some of the players from school but when I started going I was the only girl involved and the first comment was, "Who brought a f***ing woman along to watch a football game?" Then I started bringing the half-time oranges and that calmed them down a bit. As secretary I'm now accepted, and if they ever have any problems I'm the unofficial agony aunt.'

She has also persuaded other women to watch games. 'I enjoy watching the matches, but it took a few months to persuade other wives and girlfriends to come along. It's more like a club for them now.'

Posh Spice may find David Beckham irresistible in his shorts, but, despite living with the goalkeeper, Joanne wasn't turned on by her first sight of Stewart's body in lycra cycling shorts and a dayglo jersey.

'Stewart has got a nice pair of legs, but in goal his shorts are too long so you can only see his knees. When he was playing up front he did look quite fit in his kit though. Some of them have got nice legs but others you think, Oh dear . . .'

Caroline Waters is the fiancée of midfielder Colin Jobling and more of a football widow: 'I get told to come along. I'm dragged out of bed!' Does she find the lads in shorts sexy? 'That's Colin over there, the fat lardy one in the middle! We come here to talk about babies, weddings, shopping and chocolate,' she laughs.

It seems the stars of the Flying Pig are less sex gods and more footballing Teletubbies to their female fans.

And what's Colin like after the match? 'He'll say his knee or groin hurts and ask me to give him a massage. If he's got a groin strain I just tell him to shut up and stop being a girl. Colin is a wimp really. He wears about five T-shirts when it's cold.'

'There goes the wedding!' comments fellow footballing partner Tracey.

Anita Jackson is married to Flying Pig manager Michael 'Wacko' Jackson. 'You can't ever say it's just a game to him . . .' she laughs.

Tracey is married to Steve Gilbey. 'He's the one who's just been booked. But he's a big pussy cat really. He worries about being cold with no gloves or coat. Steve didn't speak to Mike once after he had a go at him.'

'Mike thinks that if he's horrible to them it makes them want to prove him wrong,' says Anita Jackson. 'He says, "There's always room for improvement."'

This causes general merriment as the likely lasses imitate their spouses in dumb voices: 'Did you see my goal . . . you never watch me play . . . you were all talking . . .'

Trouble and strife

For the performer on the pitch there's nothing worse than cracking a 30 yarder into the top corner of the net, running along the touchline to your biggest fan and discovering that she's lost in a book.

Even Liz Hurley spent much of the game reading when she watched Hugh Grant play in a charity match at the Royal Hospital in London in 1988. 'It was fun seeing all those little legs running around. Hugh shot a goal or whatever it is boys do. Really I find football quite dull. I certainly wasn't cheering; most of the time I was reading my book. But luckily the Royal Hospital is just off the King's Road so it's near the shops and I went shopping afterwards with my sister.'

George Ward, manager of Milldean, knows the reading scenario only too well. 'My ex-wife only came to watch me once and I went down with an elbow in the face. There was blood pouring everywhere, the trainer rushing on, and I had to be carried off. When I went over to see her, she was still reading her book. She hadn't even noticed!'

An uneasy truce was reached. 'We agreed that if I didn't mention the score she wouldn't tell me what a waste of time football is.' On another occasion, George arrived to pick her up from a dinner party with a black eye, having been elbowed in the face during a match.

'All her friends were squash-playing types and it was in the days when football was seen as all thuggery. She said, "Don't you dare tell them you've injured yourself playing football. Say you've been playing cricket." I had to convince everyone I'd been hit by a bouncer!'

Some footballing widows exert their own penalties. 'After fifteen years my wife has decided she wants a bit of time to herself as well, and I have to take my two daughters with me every Sunday,' says Martin Bester of Yeovil side the Masons Arms. 'I have to hope that where we're playing there's a park. She's getting her own back on me.'

In fact, this is a useful approach to solving problems, says Denise Knowles of Relate (formerly the Marriage Guidance

Council). 'One couple I counselled solved their problems in this way. It gave the wife time alone and meant the man felt involved with his children – and he commented that Sunday dinners had never been so good because without the children his wife had time to cook them properly!'

As most footballers still seem incapable of washing their own kit, one of the easiest ways for a football widow to take revenge is to refuse to wash those sweaty socks. A few vengeful women have even cut up their men's kit.

'One man had to keep rushing out to buy new shorts and jockstraps every Sunday as his wife wouldn't wash them,' says Knowles. 'Another wife said she wouldn't wash mud-caked kit as she gave up washing dirty nappies years ago.'

Every weekend the sex wars continue. Unwashed kits are left festering in utility rooms and a myriad frustrated partners declare that there's nothing so stupid as eleven men chasing after an inflated bladder. If marriage is a game of two halves, then football is definitely 1-0 up before the interval.

Knowles says that a lot of partners become jealous of their men playing football because of insecurity. 'They feel they come behind football and that he's having a good time while they're not. There's also a lot of disagreements about the effects of the game, when the man can't go for a walk because he's tired and got aches and pains. What a lot of women often don't realise is that they too can do a sport or two on nights in the week and their husbands are usually quite happy with this.'

Of course, it helps if you occasionally show some appreciation of your semi-bereaved partner. At the now-defunct West Coast Armadillos in London they once presented a player's wife with the Player-of-the-Year award. She'd had to suffer her husband playing on Saturdays and Sundays and training twice a week, and, as none of the players had performed particularly well that season, this unsung heroine seemed the natural choice. She took the award home and proudly placed it on her mantelpiece.

Even players without regular girlfriends soon discover that women can interfere with their Sunday morning pleasure. 'It can often be difficult getting the younger players out on a

Sunday morning, because they're having a bit of nookie for the first time in their lives,' confesses Windy Millers' David Lane.

Most Sunday league players will have experienced the dilemma at some stage of their career. They've scored at a Saturday night party, they're lying hungover in bed with a woman who looks like Zoë Ball and – oh my God – it's 10 am and you have to be at the match for an 11 o'clock kick-off twenty miles away.

Can you possibly let down ten team-mates? Invariably the response is, 'Sorry, love, I've gotta play football!' as the errant player runs down the stairs and what seemed a perfect love match a few hours earlier is now strictly a game of one half. Those who do play extra-time in bed often find themselves banished from the side for weeks – and never make the same mistake again.

It can affect your game too. Despite what George Best claims, it does seem that too much sex can ruin your ball control. Defender Chris Ashmore was named Git of the Game after returning from his sixteen-day honeymoon in Canada with bride Jennie. Ashmore's first game on his return to Ilkeston, Notts, saw him score an incredible three own goals in Ilford's 5-3 defeat of Breadsall. He took some terrible stick from his team-mates and manager George Harris fumed, 'His brain was in the bedroom.' Jennie had little sympathy for the hapless defender. 'I might have worn him out but that's what honeymoons are for. He should have had more stamina.'

Too sexy for their shorts

But, thankfully, at least some women are now accepting the importance of football. After the success of Nick Hornby's *Fever Pitch*, single wannabe Bridget Joneses might even follow you to the match.

Anne Coddington, author of *One of the Lads* (Harper-Collins), a history of women in football, says: 'Football has lost its image of being a dirty racist game where men kick the hell out of each other. The 1990 World Cup with Pavarotti helped, as did stadia changes. Women are more aware of the game because it's so high profile with crossover programmes like *Fantasy Football.*

'Footballers are on the catwalk and Ian Walker was a male centrefold. With foreign players like Ruud Gullit and Zola here, it's associated with aesthetics more. And you see plenty of girls wearing Adidas sports shirts now. When the Spice Girls started, Sporty Spice was stuck at the back, but now she's far more prominent. Young girls see you can be sporty and sexy at the same time, whereas, before football, was considered un-feminine.'

Football has never been so sexy or glamorous. Babes and footballers are now matching accessories. The tabloids have at various times salivated over Posh Spice and David Beckham, Dani Behr and Les Ferdinand, Ulrika Jonsson and Stan Collymore and Louise and Jamie Redknapp. Anthea Turner left husband Peter Powell for Grant Bovey, a man who sells football videos and once made a £30 million bid for Nottingham Forest. And even football fans are now seen as objects of desire. In the film of *Fever Pitch*, baldy anorak Nick Hornby is portrayed by sex god Colin 'Mr Darcy' Firth.

Only, has this phenomenon trickled down into the Sunday leagues? Perhaps it has, for even linesmen now have their fans. Nikki Davies watches her husband Simon run the line for the Sun in Reading. 'Once he was ill in bed, and he complained because I went to watch the lads and then spent all Sunday lunchtime in the pub with them. What a cheek! I carried the kit bag and a bucket of tepid water and once I nearly got into a fight after a terrible tackle from an opposition player.

'It beats antique fairs. Sometimes I was the only fan. My brother's a runner so I do have some experience of sports massage for cramps and the players often insisted I warmed them up. There was one who always used to claim to have cramp . . .

'A couple of them were nice young fellows and I did get to massage their calves which was quite sexy. When they were injured, I sprayed on the Ralgex, so I saw a couple of pert young buttocks. I once sprayed too far up and caused some pain in a tender area. Simon promised the top scorer an unprintable sexual service from me, but I had to explain to him at the awards ceremony that this was just a joke. He looked quite disappointed.'

But having your partner on the sidelines can cause distractions for some players, as Jim Brodie, chairman of Colinthians in Birmingham, remembers. 'A few years ago we had this lad called Pete whose girlfriend always came along to watch. Whenever he scored, he'd run over to kiss her. We were all old men and he was the only one of us with a young girlfriend. So, whenever anyone else scored, we started running over to kiss her. She ran away for a bit, but I think she was most grateful when I did finally get hold of her.'

That's one problem which Posh Spice has not, as yet, had to face – being chased down the touchline by a slobbering Gary Pallister.

And some players probably wish their wives were still football widows. At Milldean, Jackie Knox, the wife of former club secretary Barry Knox, started to attend matches but showed a little too much enthusiasm.

'She once threw a cup of coffee over our ex-manager when he asked her not to talk to her brother until he'd finished his half-time talk,' confesses Barry. 'At another game she was running the line and was asked by the ref to quieten down. She told him to "just f**king get on with it" and was booked, so the referee threatened to abandon the game unless she left the touchline. But at least she likes football – I don't have the problems of the other players!'

But the true test of the soccer girlfriend is if she turns up on a windswept morning on Hackney Marshes in London. A search among the pitches on a typical Sunday muddy Sunday revealed that more and more women are watching their partners play.

There can be few more traditionally male environments than Hackney Marshes. As they wait for the kick-off, some players even have cans of beer as they stand by their cars having a fag. Others are buying breakfast from the burger bar outside the changing rooms. Steamed broccoli and pasta it ain't. Sports nutrition is for wimps. Everywhere there are groups of men with bags and harassed secretaries talking into mobile phones.

As they run on to the pitch it's not uncommon to see players in their kit stop to urinate by the newly planted trees. The grass is damp. A grey river meanders between the pitches. Endless white goalposts stretch towards the horizon.

But even here some women have penetrated into the male maelstrom on the Marshes. The Trafalgar Colts are being watched by Chiarina Fernandez and Nicola Hammond. 'I've got Italian and Spanish blood which is why I love football,' says 25-year-old Chiarina. 'I started watching my brother play. My boyfriend Paul enjoys it when I watch him, apart from when I tell him he could improve his ball control or that he's not running into space. But he knows I'm talking sense really. He's even asked me to talk to them at half-time, but normally I relay my thoughts on the game through him as boys won't listen to a girl. I was a linesman for one game, but I gave it up because I got so much abuse.'

Does she find Paul sexy in his kit? 'I think it's the man inside that's sexy, not the kit itself. And they're not exactly Ginolas. There are a few too many beer guts on view. My favourite player is Maldini and there's no one to compare with him out there.'

Nicola, 21, is married to Terry, the side's player-manager, and watches games with their two-year-old son Jake. Their eyes first met across a crowded game of football in the school playground. 'His class were the only one that would let me play with them. At first I used to watch him in school matches. My family have always liked football. I like to see them do well and I like a good fight as long as no one gets hurt. I tell Terry what he's done wrong after the game and he gets the hump. Sometimes he does appreciate it though, when I tell him what he should have done when he received the ball. Do I like him in his kit? Oh yeah, especially when he's all sweaty!'

At half-time Chiarina decides not to relay her tactical advice through Paul, but takes the lads to one side herself. 'Come on, boys! That goal was offside but you're playing well – just keep playing football. And don't keep going down one side – switch the ball from right to left . . .' And amazingly – given the laddish nature of footballers – they all listen and take it in.

On another pitch, Tracey Hallson and her son Alex are watching Tracey's boyfriend Leroy Baxter play in goal for Stanford. 'I hated it before I started watching Leroy but I love it now. It's a really good game. I still don't watch it on TV, but here it's really exciting.'

But the ultimate dedication is surely shown by Julie Buckingham, who is sitting behind the goal on crutches with a broken leg watching Downham play, accompanied by her boyfriend David, who's the side's injured goalkeeper. Her broken leg was the result of 'tripping over after one too many cans'. She's so entered the spirit of Sunday league football that she and David are drinking cans of lager on the touchline. 'I won an award from the club for being the best supporter,' says Julie proudly. 'I've always liked team games and I used to play women's rugby for Neath. I really enjoy the team spirit and I help with the medical kit too. David definitely looks good in his shorts. It's not the legs, it's more to do with the arse really. He's got a nice bottom.'

So it's true – park footballers really are too sexy for their shorts. If you can get your partner to watch the game and she enjoys it, you've got a result. Sadly, some women are still unconvinced by muddy touchlines, and keeping her indoors happy remains the ultimate goal of most players. Many men are still fighting a never-ending battle to convince their partners that they are not obsessed and some things really are more important than Sunday morning football – like the Sky game in the afternoon.

HOW TO KEEP YOUR PARTNER HAPPY

DO

Encourage her to take up sport herself

Offer to take the kids with you

Invite her to watch the game

Agree to be home for the odd Sunday lunch

Accept her tactical advice

Wash your own kit

Present her with a Player-of-the-Year trophy for
   sacrifices beyond the call of duty

Agree that all those injuries are your own fault

Tell her that you really will retire next season

If necessary, agree to tell her friends that your injuries
   are from cricket, bowls or polo and definitely not
   football

DON'T

Spend hours in the pub after the game

Dump the team kit by the washing machine for her to do

Go out for a bottle of milk and end up on a tour in Belgium

Be too tired to perform between the sheets

Say 'football' if she asks you to choose between football
   and her

Wake her up with Sunday morning ring-rounds

Get on the wrong train and ask her to pick you up from
   the wrong city after a boozy tour

Claim you'll do the DIY after the game and then fall
   asleep

Get annoyed if she agrees to watch you and spends 90
   minutes reading a book

17 The Boys from Brazil

'Baldiniho is scythed down on the edge of the area and this is surely free-kick territory for those magical Brazilians, Trevor. Will they play it in the air to Vertigo or will one of the dead-ball specialists have a crack from 35 yards? I can see Fellatio fancies a go; there's also Wrightiniho and Billio lining up ... Bazziniho leaps over the ball and it's Billio ... Oh, what a goal! I don't think you'll see a better struck ball in the Aylesbury Sunday Football Combination this season, Trevor.'

If you received a video of Brazil's superb 1970 World Cup-winning side as a Christmas or birthday gift then return it immediately, for the Brazilians, albeit slightly fatter than in their prime, can now be found playing in division four of the Aylesbury Sunday Football Combination.

It was all the idea of a 32-year-old 'Brazilian' called Wrightiniho, aka manager Steve Wright. 'A group of us were playing for the White Horse in Whitchurch and we were all getting a bit old, so we decided to get together with a load of drinkers who hadn't played in years to form the Brazil 70 side to guarantee us a game,' says Wrightiniho. 'We're connoisseurs of football and beer. We had a discussion about which was the greatest side we'd ever seen and came up with Brazil in 1970, so we decided to name ourselves after them.'

By day, midfielder/goalkeeper Wrightiniho sells hearing aids for a living, which some followers might think appropriate, considering the age of the 30-something side. But, whatever your age, you never lose true skill.

Brazil might have had Rivelino, Tostao, Carlos Alberto and Jairzinho, but the Aylesbury outfit can match them with the likes of Mad Doggio, Baldiniho, Bazziniho and Wrightiniho. And, to confuse the opposition even more, these names are attached to the back of their classic 1970 Brazil shirts.

Baldiniho is so named because defender Chris Hudspith is thinning on top. E-I-Adio is a play on Adrian Biggs' name, while in similar vein Dave Phillipson has become Phillipiniho, Barry Phipps is now Bazziniho, Mark 'Bondy' Jones is Bondiniho ('although nobody knows why he's called Bondy in the first place'), Pat Wilson is Paddiho and Mark 'Billy' Butcher is Billio.

Other Brazilian nicknames are a little more risqué. 'Fellatio is a lad called Steve. He's married with a son, but in his youth he was a bit promiscuous. It's quite embarrassing for him now,' says Wrightiniho of the star who presumably gives a blow-by-blow account of each game. Fellatio has even been known to wear his Brazilian shirt when watching his beloved West Ham play.

'Sturdio has big thick legs and we used to call him Sturdy, so it came from that. Kerry Gardener is called Bisto as he lives in Bicester and our tallest player is called Vertigo,' explains Wrightiniho. 'We don't know why Tony Forchione is called Chillio, it's something to do with him being an Italian. He's also known as Tony Angles, because he fires them in from all angles. Mad Doggio is our goalkeeper Neil. He's a nice bloke but he's got a temper on him. He used to be our centre half and when we put him in goal he punched at every cross – he likes punching. He chose the name and we didn't dare argue.'

But no discussion of Brazil could fail to mention Edson Arantes Do Nascimento. And, like that great Brazil side of 1970, the Aylesbury version also revolves around their brilliant number 10, Pele. Emerson once said that he would never play in Brazil again because, 'In Brazil you have to kill a lion each day. For six months you are Pele, then two bad games and you are nobody.' But he'd clearly never seen Brazil 70 play, for 28-year-old Ian Aiston is Pele every week.

'Ian's the club joker. He's not called Pele because he's good, but because he thinks he's good and everything revolves around him. He is quite skilful, I suppose, but he can't run,' explains Wrightiniho.

Pele has been known to arrive at the club with a Bible and start quoting the gospels before matches. Pele's first attempt at Bible-bashing allegedly resulted in Brazil playing well despite suffering a crushing 9-0 defeat. The next week, they actually had their first-ever victory, which can only be put down to divine intervention, claim the lads. For the club's last match of the season in division three, Pele arrived wearing holiday gear, sunglasses, Bermuda shorts, a big wide tie and sandals.

'When I'm up against opposition players I often say, "I bet you never thought you'd be marking Pele!" and they have a good laugh,' says Pele.

Pele is a self-confessed 'big lad' weighing fifteen stone, but he's not afraid to imitate his illustrious namesake. 'I jig around with the ball a bit and try nutmegs. The lads look at me and think, He's never going to do it, but sometimes the flicks come off. I've never tried to score from the halfway line, but I did score once in a friendly with a twenty-yard lob. We played the first half wearing black Brazilian wigs, but I'd taken it off by the time I scored.'

Inevitably there can be some confusion when referees book Brazil players. 'Luckily the ref who booked Pele knew him, so he didn't have to turn him round and check the name on his shirt. In fact, he then started asking Pele how his family were keeping,' laughs Wrightiniho. Pat Wilson, aka Paddiho, also doubles up as the club linesman known as Linho.

The lads are now local celebrities and are often approached in the pub by people saying, 'You play for Brazil, don't you?' And of course, no Brazilian side would be complete without the camera panning to Brazilian babes in the crowd clad in carnival gear. Cherie Wilson, fiancée of Bazziniho (aka Barry Phipps) and daughter of Paddiho, was asked to become secretary. This woman really does have yellow and green blood.

'I love the team spirit and watching the side progress. I've been to every single game with my seat and flask. They keep asking where my fishing rod is!' says Cherie. 'I won the Supporter-of-the-Year award and at the presentation they asked me to be secretary. Being a woman probably helps – I just tell 'em to pay their subs and they don't argue with me.

'I'm also the trainer so I get to run on with a massive medical bag – but the sponge usually gets them up.' She is now so accepted by the side that she has earnt the ultimate blokeish accolade – they sometimes call her Cheziniho.

Pele's brother Kevin 'Aistiniho' Aiston even turned the Brazil 70 side into a political party, the Birthday Party, at the May election, and appointed himself foreign secretary. 'We're all for coming out of Europe and doing all our business with Brazil. Nuts, football and Ronnie Biggs, that's all we're interested in,' declared Aistiniho. Carpenter Barry 'Bazziniho' Phipps was appointed cabinet maker and pub landlord Stan Dey was naturally heritage secretary. Education secretary Paddy 'Paddiho' Wilson was adamant: 'We want Blur not Blair.' The local paper printed a picture of the entire cabinet-in-waiting with pints in hand, but sadly the country opted for New Labour instead.

Drinkus, Get Pissus, Playi Footballus

The side played its first match at the start of the 1996–97 season, inspired by the motto of 'Drinkus, Get Pissus, Playi Footballus'. Brazil 70's campaign was not quite as successful as Brazil's World Cup-winning side. Initial progress was slow with nine defeats in nine games, 53 goals conceded and only three scored.

'The problem was that half the side had never kicked a ball in anger in their life. We wanted to start off in division four, but on the basis that the other half of the side had played for the White Horse in division two, we were put in division three,' says Wrightiniho.

In the side's first two seasons, there have been some disciplinary problems with the brilliant but temperamental Brazilians. Flair players with Latin blood have never been good at time keeping – particularly so when the Brazilians have been quaffing unfamiliar English ale. 'Some players could be seen balancing on two bar stools singing tuneful melodies on Saturday night, yet on Sunday morning resembled nine-month-old babies learning to walk,' claims Wrightiniho. Bazziniho,

Paddiho, Sturdio, Linho and Cheziniho were all found guilty on grounds of diminished responsibility and suffered £1 club fines after pub trials.

For Bazziniho there was a double humiliation when a £1 fine was accompanied by all-round ridicule for his excuse – he claimed to have been late because he'd been slightly tipsy at a barn dance. It was left to Wrightiniho to give the naive youngster a fatherly caveat on how to handle the media in the next issue of *Brazil Nuts*. 'A word of advice for Bazziniho: when giving excuses it would be more acceptable to say that you have been to an all-night rave rather than a barn dance.'

But Bazziniho escaped a club fine after arriving late for the 9-0 defeat at Weston Turville on unusual grounds. 'The management decided to waive the customary fine due to the fact that the night before Bazziniho had managed to walk the entire length of the White Horse bar including pillars, flaps, and pumps – a truly amazing feat,' explained a spokesman for Brazil 70's Disciplinary Committee. Perhaps he should be charged by the FA with bringing drinking into repute.

During one 0-3 defeat at the hands of the Old Plough and Harrow Reserves, a frustrated Paddiho was even moved to shout, 'For Christ's sake, am I invisible?' To which E-I-Adio replied, 'Who said that?'

Throughout their tentative first steps in top-class football, Brazil were supported by their loyal fan Travelling Pete. 'He did have a car, but I think he pranged it. So now he always has bus timetables in his pocket and can tell you the time of the next bus to anywhere in the county. He's a bit of an anorak,' says Wrightiniho. One incident where Travelling Pete arrived late at a strange ground, bus timetables in hand, has now entered club mythology. Travelling Pete told a groundsman, 'I can't find Brazil.' The groundsman replied, 'That's because you're in England, mate!'

But true class will always out. Football history was made when Brazil 70 recorded their first victory, an epic 3-2 win over Rivets Reserves. Pele's Bible reading before the game had worked. The goals, scored by Tony 'Chillio' Forchione (2) and Aistiniho were celebrated by a team samba that was even more impressive than Aylesbury United's 'duck walk'.

'We thought about doing the Faustino Asprilla celebration when he ran to the corner flag and picked it up against Metz in the UEFA Cup, but we were all too knackered to make it to the corner flag,' said Wrightiniho.

In a 3-2 home defeat to Weston Turville Reserves, Bazziniho celebrated his first goal of the season with an astonishing series of cartwheels, somersaults and gymnastic movements. After such celebrations he felt it necessary to spend the next ten minutes sitting on the sidelines.

Sadly, Brazil 70 were relegated at the end of the 1996–97 season. But by mid-season 1997–98 the Brazilian magic was beginning to pay off with Baldiniho and Co. near the top of division four. The Brazilians even hammered Killrush 9-0. Alas, the excitement was too much for Sturdio, who became the first Brazilian to throw up after a game, although it was probably due more to Saturday night's liquid motivation rather than excitement.

But division four has started to see the best of the magical Brazilians as the side has maintained a position in the top six. The lads have been celebrating their goals with cartwheels from Bazziniho, sambas, congas, running round corner flags and Brazilian hand linking and mock baby-cradling routines. They've even tried a collective Harry Enfield old newsreel comedy footballer routine and Aistiniho and Bazziniho have performed a strut your funky stuff 1970s disco dance. It's also now a club tradition that whenever a penalty is successfully converted, the scorer has his shorts pulled down – presumably to reveal his Brazil nuts.

Brazilian benders

And of course the side's free-kick routines are deadly. Rivelino would have been dumbfounded at some of the efforts that have graced the pitches of Aylesbury. 'We did have one free kick that swerved,' remembers Wrightiniho, who also edits the club's *Brazil Nuts* fanzine. 'It was taken by Billio who's seventeen stone. He went out and bought some Predator boots – God knows why – and hit the post, but he's never done it again. The thing is he can't kick it straight normally, so it's an advantage when taking free kicks.'

However, most Brazilian efforts from long range still tend to go the way of a 'chip' from Chillio, who in trying to execute a perfect chip over the opposition goalkeeper, managed to knock the ball over the bar, then over a 30-foot fence and into the back garden of a house, smashing a large flowerpot and causing scenes of Victor Meldrew-style irritation among the residents.

During a 9-0 defeat at Weston Turville in the relegation season, even Wrightiniho let fly with a 30-yard effort and grazed the bar – that's the kids' climbing bar located 40 yards behind the goal. Another memorable piece of Brazilian magic came during a 0-3 home defeat to Quarrenden Athletic, when Baldiniho knocked the ball past an opponent, in true Pele style. 'Only Baldiniho decided that if he couldn't get round him he'd jump on his back and pretend he was a horse,' chuckles Wrightiniho.

Which is not to say that the boys from Brazil have yet given up hopes of making the grade at the very highest level. The Middlesbrough manager Bryan Robson is already rumoured to be taking an interest in their exploits. After the departure of Emerson, Robson went out of his way to emphasise, 'I'd certainly sign another Brazilian. It has not put me off them – definitely not.' And the only signing-on fee Bazziniho and co. would require would be a few pints in Middlesbrough's hostelries.

And lest Glenn Hoddle thinks England will have it easy in international football, his boys might yet have to face an unexpected threat. 'We haven't given up hope of receiving the call from the Brazilian manager Mario Zagallo,' says a hopeful Pele. 'That would cause some divided loyalties for the England fans, but we'd certainly play our hearts out for the famous green and yellow shirts.'

18 Honey, I Shrunk the Kits

'Giggsy, you're washing the kit . . .' announces Alex Ferguson, pointing to a sweaty mass of red and white shirts, shorts and screwed-up socks.

'But, boss, it's Keaney's turn this week!'

'I did it last week!' counters Keaney. 'What about Buttsy? It must be his turn . . .'

'He'll shrink it again,' moans Gary Pallister. 'What about you, Coley?'

'It's too heavy, man. That'll weigh down my new motor. What about Scholesy?' says Coley.

'I'm not bloody changing a £50 note into fifty pences again . . . And they won't allow Ole Gunnar Solskjaer in the launderette without his mum, so it must be Becks's turn,' reasons the ginger-haired star, as sharp at avoiding his kit-washing duties as he is in front of goal.

'I'm over at Posh Spice's place. She'll go mad if I bring home a bag full of festering kit,' pleads Becks. 'And the utility room's full of her stage gear.'

'All right, lads, all right,' announces the weary Ferguson. 'You win. We have won 6-0 this week, so I'll take the kit home and get the missus to do it . . .'

The Old Trafford dressing room erupts into cheers and an impromptu conga around the muddy kit.

If only Alex Ferguson had the problems of most Sunday league managers then we'd discover his true mettle as a boss. Coaching the side to the FA Carling Premiership is relatively easy compared to getting the kit washed every week.

There can be no more emotive topic in Sunday football. The best side can be a goal down before they leave the changing

rooms if they're wearing last week's rancid kit, still full of stale
sweat after the fat goalkeeper forgot to go to the launderette.

How can you perform well when your kit looks like a junior
side's cast-offs? Many sides took to the pitch wearing bumster
shorts long before Alexander McQueen made them trendy,
unaware that they were potential fashion icons. Indeed, were
McQueen ever to adopt Sunday league couture, with its white
shirts dyed pink, gut-hugging mini-shirts stretched over ripples
of wobbling flesh, ripped shorts and sweaty fragrance, then he
could create his most sensational designs yet.

McQueen might have been proud of the way Brookmans
Park adopted workerist chic. 'We've had the classic hot wash
where our orange shirts come out brown and the socks are like
ankle socks,' says secretary Jeff Spencer. 'But the biggest kit
fiasco we had was when a lad called Dave washed the kit and
left half of it in the airing cupboard. We were playing away and
only had seven shirts, but the home team managed to find four
orange workman's bibs, the sort of thing British Rail workers
on the line wear. So four of us had to run around in these
sleeveless workmen's bibs, which was pretty embarrassing.
Dave won our Nightmare-of-the-Year trophy for that.'

Players can ruin the kit in a bewildering number of ways.
They can't even make it easy by unravelling the socks. They are
to launderettes and washing machines what Peter Stringfellow
is to celibacy. There is no such thing as safe socks. Brookmans
Park's Jeff Spencer has been a victim of the laundry lock-out, a
common feature of footballing life. 'One of our players left the
kit in the launderette on a Friday, didn't get it on a Saturday
and then spent all Sunday morning trying unsuccessfully to get
the owner up. We had to use the second team kit eventually.'

As player and secretary of Milldean, veteran George Ward
has seen just about every conceivable cock-up on the kit front.
'You can't trust the players to do anything,' he sighs. 'Three of
them forgot to sign their registration forms despite filling them
in, so we started the season with three unregistered players.

'As for washing the kit, only the other week a lad called
Swindon refused to wash it. It was really muddy and horrible
and weighed a ton. He said, "If you give it to me it'll come back

in the same state." He was worried he couldn't get a service wash, but I said, "I'm not doing it." He said we needed a proper secretary, and the kit is probably still festering on the floor somewhere!'

But if the kit does get washed, be careful with your choice of conditioner, lads, for even the most macho of sides can be undone by a poncey niff emanating from their armpits. 'One bloke had got his wife to wash it and she'd used perfume,' exclaims Ward. 'It smelt terrible. It made your eyes water just putting it on. Everyone was going, "Who put this stuff on our bloody kit?" She'd probably put it on to wind us all up . . .'

'We've had a red and white strip came back pink because they've washed it too hot,' continues Ward. 'And in the old days when we all wore little shorts, they'd come back shrunk, so you'd have these blokes with big fat thighs trying to put them on and they'd look like bikini bottoms.'

The most recent Milldean mishap involved the new fashion for adhesive numbers. 'We have these stick-on numbers and this lad must have boiled them. All the numbers came off; they were on the front and on the back of the shirts. It was like a dyslexic football team.'

The furthest Ward has ever had to go to trace the kit is from London to Skegness. 'A few of the players had gone to Skegness for the weekend and some of the others had tagged along. Only eight players turned up in the morning and everyone was going, "Who's got the kit?" Someone said, "Ask Swindon where the kit is."'

'Only it turned out Swindon was in Skegness. We phoned him and woke him up after he'd had a night on the booze. He told us it was in his garage. So we all went round to the garage and it was covered in security cameras and alarms. We thought, No way are we touching that or we'll end up inside. With eight men and no kit we decided to call it off. But Swindon acted like it was our fault, and he got the hump with us for phoning when he'd got a hangover.'

Every side has its tale of shrunken kit. Denis Wilson of Harold Wood Hospital FC in Essex recalls, 'Once one of our supporters tried to do us a favour by washing the kit. He put it all on a hot wash and shrunk everything! He came in very sheepishly, put the kit bag down and wandered off.' From then on it was men against boys. 'It all looked like tank tops and bikini tops. We had to play for four weeks in it. It was skin tight. We're a large side and had to peel our shirts off!'

Wilson has other kit problems too. 'My wife refused to do the kit after the washing machine broke because it was full up with mud. It cost me £200 for a new machine. I thought, That's the last time I try to save £2 a week by doing it at home! One of the nurses does our kits now in exchange for a crate of wine.'

Carl Ridyard of AFC Mapleleaf in Newark has suffered stick from his wife, who's clearly found the kit a fatal distraction: 'My missus and the manager's missus normally wash the kit. My wife's always hassling me about the socks not being turned out and she threatens not to do it when it's muddy. She's given up ironing it in protest.

'It causes arguments, but the missus does get £5 a week from club funds for doing it. I always tell her, "The washing machine does it, not you!" She should be grateful for the privilege of washing our kit, really, though she'll kill me for saying that.'

Manchester Maccabi's secretary Brenda Davidson despairs of her male charges. 'Each player takes it in turns to go to the launderette. We have opened the bag to the stench of what's supposed to be clean kit. They're horrible, men! Sometimes people have turned up without the kit because they've forgotten the launderette wasn't open on a Sunday and we've had to borrow another kit and kick off late. I have to do the sewing as well. We've got a player who regularly bursts his pants . . .'

And talking of broken shorts, Steve Hurst, a former star striker with the Civil Service Third XI, recalls some particularly dilapidated kit. 'If you were last to arrive you got the split shorts. They were completely open around the crotch. It was like wearing a kilt!'

'A memorable moment was when we took the kit out of the bag before the game and there was a pair of women's knickers in it!' recalls Steve. 'The guy who washed it certainly got some stick about what he'd been getting up to after that.'

And it's not just the kit that players can destroy through their ineptitude at domestic chores. Goal nets have been known to suffer too. One summer, while his wife was out and unable to complain about the mud, Phil Colver of Colinthians in Birmingham decided to wash his side's goal nets. 'Only when the season started my team-mates found we had a problem: the nets had shrunk. Somehow they put them up for the first game. But despite later attempts to put them up, they just weren't big enough. I had to fork out £60 to buy a new set. If only my wife had been there to recommend a low-temperature wash.'

Colver then lent the shrunken nets to a colleague, who lent them to another player whose car was stolen with the useless nets in the boot. 'So if anybody in the West Midlands area tries to sell you a pair of used white nets check that they fit,' suggests Colver.

Washing the kit plays such an important role in the team's campaign that it inevitably features in the end-of-season awards. Mike Pattenden of London side Millbank won the Worst Excuse For Forgetting The Kit medal. 'I didn't even have an excuse. I'd just forgotten it. We had to borrow another team's disgusting kit – and we got stuffed in it.'

At the Wiltshire side Jesters, the manager's tolerant wife Mags always washes the kit. 'We decided to give her an award, as she always does a good job,' says Jesters secretary Bill Liddiard. 'She does it out of love for her husband, not us. Mags has threatened not to do it if the socks aren't turned out, but I think the manager just gives her a few extra Bacardi and cokes. Everyone else got trophies and tankards, and then Mags received this great big wrapped parcel. She probably thought it was a cup, but it was a giant box of Persil! She took it quite well, really.'

Andy Taylor, secretary of the New Inn Sidley, adopts the unreconstructed male option with the dirty kit and gives it to the missus.

'We take it in turns to wash the kit, but really only about six of us do it, and then it's usually the wives. The lads who live on their own aren't much good. One single player put the blue shorts in with the white shirts and we had to play in light blue shirts for two seasons! He's been banned from ever washing the kit again.

'I know what a washing machine looks like, but I'm not sure how it works, so I leave it to the wife,' confesses Taylor. 'She's always complaining about the mud and how it weighs five times heavier when it comes back after the game.'

Ask a footballer to fix a hi-fi system or install software on a PC and it's easy. Put him in front of a washing machine and, to quote Ossie Ardiles, his legs go all trembly.

'We get all the usual excuses from the lads when they turn up with last week's sweaty kit, like, "My washing machine's broken down" and, "My mum's away,"' says Taylor. 'One week we were two shirts short. The lad who was supposed to be washing them had been spotted in town in midweek wearing them as leisurewear, which is pretty sad really, and he'd forgotten to put them back!' Or maybe he was just a fashion victim ten years ahead of his time.

We can only admire the ways men contrive to abuse their kits. Some of the special effects, like melting shirts, would be envied by most horror film producers. Perfidious Albion in London had endured a terrible kit for two and a half seasons. Hugh Jones still shivers at the memory: 'It was dirt cheap and the guy who bought it hadn't thought about the sizes. Some of the shorts looked like they'd been nicked from the fourth year at school and the shirts either made us look like Michelin Man or dwarves, and unfortunately the small shirts tended to accentuate the curves of middle age.'

Salvation came with a beautiful new blue professional-looking kit. 'But after our third game in it we gave it to one of the players to wash,' sighs Jones. 'He left it to dry on the radiators at his flat while he was at work and one of the radiators must have been hotter than usual. On three of the shirts the seams holding the sleeves on had melted away, so the sleeves fell off. We were left with three shirts that looked like tank tops. The player involved manages a branch of Habitat now, so he must have some organisational ability, but we'd never trust him to wash the kit again.'

Football, it's a wash of two cycles.

WASHING TIPS – how to just wash and go

1 – Learn how to use a washing machine.

2 – Don't put red towels or blue shorts in with white shirts.

3 – Turn the socks out before washing.

4 – Soak the kit in water overnight to remove mud.

5 – Don't make the wash too hot, derr-brain.

6 – Make sure the launderette is open on a Sunday morning, but try to collect it earlier if possible.

7 – Check the kit's in the car before leaving for the game, and not in Skegness.

8 – Don't wear the kit as leisurewear during the week.

9 – Don't leave any women's knickers in the kit bag, especially if they belong to another player's wife or girlfriend.

10 – If you insist on your wife/girlfriend/mum doing it, try to show them some appreciation. And don't let her put poncey conditioner in it so the lads smell all sweet.

19 Walking in a Winner Wonderland

You've been through the rebuild or die phase. You've survived the February exodus of players and that 8-1 away defeat with nine men. The club is solvent if not sober and the time has come to reward the club's stalwarts and out the man responsible for the miss of the season.

Everyone likes appreciation, and the Sunday league player is no different. An awards ceremony, held in a pub function room or social club, can help increase a club's funds, and more importantly boost team spirit and encourage wavering players to turn out in the wind and rain next season. And it's a chance for frustrated soccer widows to be given some reward for putting up with absent partners.

Even after a mediocre season, players have some medals to display. Every footballer likes to imagine he's at the Park Royal Hotel collecting the PFA Footballer-of-the-Year award presented by Bobby Charlton, even if in reality he's holding a £15 bit of plastic tat. The most hideous of football figurines on a stand, tacky shields and plastic medals will be greatly appreciated, disfiguring many a mantelpiece for decades to come.

Many of the awards are relatively conventional, such as those for the players' player of the year, the manager's player of the year and the club's top goalscorer. Another popular award is the clubman of the year. This goes to someone who isn't necessarily a great player, but is a little-appreciated hero, keeping the club going through his or her unstinting organisation and is not a sad bastard at all, honest.

But it's the alternative awards that best embody the Sunday league club spirit. Most clubs have at some time presented a

Wayne Kerr award, a Miss-of-the-Year medal or Worst Excuse For Not Washing The Kit Trophy. Chris Evans could find several years' worth of ideas for *TFI Friday* just by attending a few more footie prizegivings.

At Brookmans Park in Hertfordshire, the club's most contested prize is the Nightmare-of-the-Year trophy. 'We've had a number of contenders over the years,' says Jeff Spencer. 'I once won the Nightmare-of-the-Year trophy for conceding a goal after two and a half seconds. The opposition just kicked off and booted it over me into the net. There were 21 players and the ref all pissing themselves. As soon as it went in I thought Oh, no, that'll win the Nightmare-of-the-Year trophy.

'One of our players, John, had a double Nightmare-of-the-Year award, firstly for crashing his BMW into a ditch and still managing to get to the game, and secondly for a bizarre injury. He made a weird lunge without anyone being near him and took a massive dive like a trapeze artist, which put him out for three weeks. The person who left half our kit in the airing cupboard, forcing us to play in sleeveless orange BR workmen's bibs, was another worthy winner.'

Wide eyed and legless

Hitting the bar was the most important aspect of the season for London club Perfidious Albion. The lads came up with a Legless Performance-of-the-Year trophy, awarded to the player who had, in the opinion of the judges, best personified the traditions of after-match drinking. The trophy itself was the traditional footballer figure with his legs cut off. The club's Doing The Digging In Midfield award was a B & Q trowel lovingly mounted on a plinth.

Trophy footballer figures have been mutilated in many different and frequently obscene ways. Peter Brenner of Premier Trophies recalls: 'We've had them all, especially things like a "golden bollock" award. We have a figure with a victory laurel and one team got us to heat the figure so we could bend it over and it looked like he was, well, I'd better not say . . .'

James Goodwin, who produces trophies for Titles

Catalogues, had one side that brought in a toilet seat and asked to have it engraved in memory of a record club 0-12 defeat. It was presented to the goalkeeper who was then asked to wear it around his neck.

Of course, lavatory humour looms large. Colinthians in Birmingham once presented a box of toilet rolls to a player in honour of his pre-match warm-up in the loo, while Barry Davison of Manchester Maccabi won a trophy of a mounted backside. 'He was president of the club, but he's also a very keen cricketer,' says his wife and club secretary Brenda. 'When one of the teams reached a cup final, he missed it because he was playing cricket. The players never let him forget it.'

Often a club relies on one particular fanatical individual to keep things together, as was the case with Garnett FC, a side of post-Newcastle University students, set up thirteen years ago. 'A maths teacher called Paddy ran all three teams,' says Garnett's former secretary Richard Griffiths. 'He was the worst footballer alive, but since he's gone to the USA we've really missed him. He'd hand out tacky trophies and Player-of-the-Year shields, and it added a real fun aspect. He was nuts. He even turned our motto, "The Mighty Green and Black", into the Latin "Fortisime Pratig Nostrae". He then kept writing from the US suggesting what we should do. He even returned to watch us a few times.'

Paddy, who was also the club's statistical supremo, would present a shield to a player every time he played his 100th game for the club. (Although no one has, as yet, been awarded a testimonial.) 'He went through a period of calling us all vegetables, and I received a tankard engraved with the name Richard Radish,' says a bemused Griffiths, who despite his vegetable moniker never earnt a call-up with either the *Sun* or Graham Taylor's England.

Griffiths also tells of a trophy called the Smithy Award. It was named after the first winner and went to the biggest 'mouthy git' in the side. 'It usually went to the player with the worst dressing-room banter; the ones who'd boast about the previous night's conquests.'

The wit is not subtle, but usually effective. Ian 'Zico' Reid,

the 47-year-old star of the Flying Pig, was made painfully aware
of the passing years when he received a plastic dinosaur at the
club's alternative awards festival. A parody of an existing
award can work well. Despite having only been in existence for
two years, Brazil 70 in Aylesbury presented Paddio, the club's
oldest player/linesman, with a Lifetime Achievement award. Sir
Stanley Matthews look out. The fans mustn't be forgotten
either, be they human or canine. Hull is for heroes, and at the
Three Tuns they presented the club's supporter of the year with
a trophy plus a tin of chunky dog food for his pet and fellow
fan.

Mike Pattenden of London side Millbank recalls several
bizarre end-of-season trophies. 'We had a Most Injury Prone
award that went to the Gazza of our side, and a Biggest
Tantrum of the Season award that went to our striker, who was
so incensed at being substituted that he went on about it for the
entire journey from London to Birmingham for a West Ham
away match.'

Slaphead-of-the-Year

The mother of all awards ceremonies is held by the Windy
Millers. Planning begins four months in advance for an
audio-visual feast that would shame *Match of the Day*'s outside
broadcast crew.

'One of the committee members has got a video camera so
we tape games throughout the season and he mixes them into
a compilation,' explains secretary David Lane. 'We have a big
screen on the stage and we lead into the presentation with video
clips and spoof satellite link-ups. One year we just kept
repeating one of the lads missing from two yards! We had a
Windy Millers logo superimposed on the picture and in the
letters you can see an adult film – it took the players a time to
figure that one out!'

The Windy Millers have a bizarre selection of awards,
presented in their club at the Mile High Stadium where sealed
envelopes are opened on stage. A Crash-Test Dummy award for
a milkman player who crashed his float into a 40-yard trailer,

mounted ballet shoes for a player known as Twinkle Toes and mounted barbed wire for two girlfriends nicknamed Bitter and Twisted who don't take kindly to their lads being left out, have all been included.

'Our golden boot is a muddy leather boot mounted on a plaque with the toe sprayed gold,' continues master of ceremonies Lane. 'We had one player who was always in the toilet before every game. At the awards ceremony we presented him with a turd from a joke shop, mounted on a shield. We soaked it in water and he thought it was real! There's also a Slaphead-of-the-Year trophy, which is a giant comb with a gap in the middle where the teeth ought to be. That's quite coveted as the players get older. And we had a Happy Shopper bag mounted on a shield for a lad who's called Amos Leisurewear and is particularly atrociously dressed.

There's even a video spoof of Dame Edna Everage, called *Up Your Stairs*. 'We take the video up the stairs into one of the players' bedrooms and show the film at the awards, although that can be a bit embarrassing for some of our players, knowing their bedroom habits,' explains Lane. 'We've also presented Windy Millers caps instead of medals, although one or two players then said, "Where's my medal?"'

If this isn't enough madness, the Millers also insist on theme dress at their awards. 'We've also awarded tank tops to the worst dressed player on tour. In fact, I now charge 50 pence more for any player arriving at the awards ceremony without a tank top. One year everyone had to wear tartan, and another it was tuxedos.'

Good organisation is essential for a successful end-of-season awards ceremony. The date has to be right, for a start. Jesters FC of the Swindon Sunday League combine their awards ceremony with the FA Cup Final. As Jesters is a snooker hall there is no problem with a venue. 'We plan it six to eight weeks in advance and we like to make a day of it,' explains Bill Liddiard. 'In the morning we have a game against the team from the bar. Our lads turn out in stockings and suspenders but it's still the most competitive game of the season as no one wants to lose against the dregs from the bar.

'The players and their girlfriends then watch the FA Cup Final in the bar and at 7 pm we have the awards ceremony, with everyone dreaming they're at the FA Cup Final winners' dinner. As well as the usual Player-of-the-Year awards and speeches we like to salute those who aren't normally recognised. Mags the manager's wife received a giant packet of Persil for washing the kits last year and the treasurer received a Jesters T-shirt. Then it's a buffet and disco to follow. It makes a really good day out.'

It helps if any opening speech includes a notorious incident from the previous season, says Colinthians' Phil Colver. 'One year the chairman read out a long grovelling letter I'd written to the league trying to explain why one of our sides had turned up without a kit, how we'd gone to fetch another one and then found out that we could borrow one from the rugby club by which time the referee had decided that if the game hadn't kicked off by 2.30 it wasn't going ahead. All the lads thought it was hilarious. The chairman always picks up on an incident from the season and it's a good ice breaker.'

A skilled compere is essential, as players' acceptance speeches tend to veer from tearful Oscar-like blusterings to half-hour marathons. It's also wise to consider time limits when letting your stars unleash their artistic talents on the rest of the squad.

'One year we let Keith "Fashion Flaw" Jones, who's also known as The Gay Poet, read out his poetry at our tenth anniversary awards ceremony,' remembers David Lane of the Windy Millers. 'We started at seven and I said, "Right, five minutes, Keith." At 7.45 he was still on! I was saying, "Right, yeah, thanks, Keith," but he wouldn't wind up. He had sixteen pages, and he's going, "I've been here since day one, I've written this, I'm gonna carry on." We had some of these cardboard pea shooters on the tables and some of the younger players were firing polystyrene balls soaked in beer at him.'

In general, it's best to try to keep speeches short. 'Everyone knows that as soon as the chairman's speech ends the beer starts, so he's getting heckled all the time while he does all the boring stuff like thanking the sponsors,' says the Flying Pig's Joanne Griffiths. 'This makes him nervous and stumble over his words. So the whole thing ends up taking twice as long as it should.

'The shortest speech ever was from the winner of our Number One Supporter award, Mad Rich. He was so shocked that he just said his catchphrase, "Eat that!", poured his pint of lager over his head, sat down and chanted, "Dwight Yorke!" for the next half-hour.'

Barry Knox, former secretary of Milldean, also follows the short sharp speech rule. 'I certainly can't mention anything about the tour as all the wives and girlfriends are there. So I just do the awards, put on the Millwall record and let them all go mental.'

But however much preparation goes into speeches, the pros at the Café Royal surely don't have to put up with the kind of distractions that affected the grand prize-giving ceremony of the Sun in Reading – that is, unless Bobby Charlton suddenly develops a taste for toilet humour at next year's bash.

The evening was going well until compere Simon Davies noticed that he wasn't getting the complete attention of his audience. 'Everyone was either guffawing or looking horrified. Someone had put a white lavatory freshener from the urinals on the plate of one of our players called Madge (short for Magic) and told him it was a mint. He said it smelt as if someone had pissed over it, which caused a lot of laughter, and then proceeded to put it into his mouth, chew it and swallow it. The place was in uproar. I couldn't really follow that.'

The message is clear – if you want the lads to turn up for pre-season friendlies (which normally end with three players sent off), put on an awards bash. And maybe some clubs in the FA Carling Premiership searching for the camaraderie that money can't buy could learn from Sunday league awards ceremonies – although somehow you can't imagine Steve Bould being too keen on a tartan-clad Arsène Wenger presenting him with the Slaphead-of-the-Year trophy, Gianfranco Zola placing a pair of mounted ballet shoes on his mantelpiece or Stan Collymore celebrating the Nightmare-of-the-Year trophy by pouring a pint of lager over his head.

20 And Some People are on the Piss . . .

The Crusades were probably the medieval equivalent of the first football tour abroad. The original eleventh- and twelfth-century crusaders arrived in foreign parts ill prepared, badly organised, unable to speak the language and wearing totally unsuitable clothing, armed only with bloody great swords and a fanatical desire to take on the locals and drink their towns out of mead. And not much has changed since. Unleashing Sunday league sides on unsuspecting small towns in Europe has probably set EU plans for a federal Europe back twenty years.

After the discipline of rising early every Sunday morning throughout the season, the Sunday leaguer likes to relax on tour. At home his pre-match routine usually involves a hefty session on a Saturday night; on tour, away from the strict regime of league football, he attempts to at least double his alcohol consumption.

Not all clubs can afford to tour abroad. Many visit sleepy places like Margate or Torquay, where the weekend break is closer to the spirit of *Fawlty Towers*. It might be shrewd managerial psychology to take the team away and let them bond in discos, but the ensuing mayhem usually results in legions of footballers being permanently banned in towns and cities from John O'Groats to the English Riviera.

Money is scarce at most clubs so that means sharing rooms. Most Sunday footballers will recognise the unpleasant sensation of tripling up in bunk beds with the six-foot-six centre half in a child's five-foot-long bed. It's inevitable that tempers, sobriety and even sanity are all severely tested. Not a curfew has been left unbroken, not a fire escape left unclimbed or a landlord's daughter left unmolested all over the British Isles.

The Windy Millers once visited the sedate seaside resort of Bournemouth and the result was a predictable farce when the lads discovered that all the hotels were booked up with a conference for company executives.

'None of the hotels would let a gang of footballers stay, so I used someone's business card and explained that we were all sales reps in town for a conference,' recalls secretary David Lane. 'Although they must have wondered why all these executives were down for a conference carrying kit bags! We'd had these tour T-shirts printed and I told the lads not to put them on, but as soon as we'd booked in they all started wearing these luminous green T-shirts saying "The Nightmare Returns" in the bar. We'd crammed two or three players in each room as well, so we had to keep that quiet.

'Then some of the players were messing about in one of the rooms, throwing the fire extinguisher about, and it hit the door, knocking the handle off. They were locked in. No one could raise the alarm or the hotel would know that we'd double booked the rooms. So they had to stay there all night and in the morning climb out of the window to get out.

'We had breakfast in shifts, but they couldn't believe how many of us kept coming down the stairs!'

Another farcical Windy Millers tour was a trip to Norfolk to play an RAF side. 'We thought they'd put us up in a hotel, but instead we got a bleeding room with concrete slabs in the middle of an airfield with aircraft flying over all night. They didn't even give us sleeping bags. None of us slept at all.'

Where you stay is the key to a good tour – although it's amazing how many clubs turn up in the resort of their choice without having anything pre-booked. And even if the club does book somewhere it's got be right for the lifestyle of the Sunday leaguer.

Saracens from Coventry had previously toured Edinburgh with great success. Secretary Richard Macdonald takes up the story:

'We were playing a team from the Meadows and in one game we borrowed a couple of their players, and so we had these Scottish lads on our side saying, "Get into them jock bastards!" They took us to all their pubs afterwards and we had a great night out.'

But the next year Saracens stayed in a hostel with dire results. 'It was a church converted into a hostel for backpackers, so you couldn't make a noise after ten o'clock,' recalls Macdonald. 'We were told to get out after day one. In fact, they told us to leave Scotland! We were coming home after drinking as much as we could at a nightclub and inevitably a drunken football team makes a noise. There were complaints galore as all the backpackers abide by the rules. We must have annoyed a lot of Scandinavians and Germans. They'll never take a football team again after us. It was a big church that was all hollow, so every noise you made they could hear. There were two groups of us at each end and we could just hear each other. Every sound echoed terribly.'

Off the rails ...

London side Lokomotiv's weekend tour of Eastbourne was taken up with drinking, drinking and more drinking. So much so that the players decided to adopt shock therapy to cure their hangovers. 'It's now tradition that no matter how drunk we get we meet up in the B & B and play Quasar after breakfast,' says Brian Benson. 'The same place turned us away at night but let us in at ten in the morning when we were probably even more drunk. There's all this smoke, flashing lights and music. You see blokes sitting in the cave, shivering and being sick and shooting people as they go past. Then we go for a walk on the beach to try to recover for the lunchtime session.'

One such tour was sabotaged by that predictable cocktail of sex and violence, remembers Benson. 'It all ended in a right punch-up. One of our players, who I'll call Dave though it's not his real name, had been chatting up the landlord's daughter and not surprisingly the landlord objected. It was past closing time and we were having a lock-in. Only things got out of hand and a scuffle developed between our lad and the landlord.

'Dave got a black eye, but not before this girl had given him a love-bite. When he got home he had to explain to his wife how he'd got both a black eye and a love-bite. In the end he told her that he'd got in a fight and someone had bit him! He blamed it all on a player called Andy, who's a quiet lad and had absolutely nothing to do with it. Dave's wife never spoke to Andy again.

'After that, whenever Dave got booked he'd give Andy's name – so Andy lost out twice. The following year Dave was involved in the same sort of incident and his wife stopped him playing for us.'

A weekend in Margate provided even more mishaps for one Lokomotiv star who must have felt like John Cleese in *Clockwise*. 'We were all delayed by Romano, whose car had broken down,' continues Benson, 'because we have a rule that everyone has to be there before we start to spend the club's £600. Everyone was desperate to start drinking, but eventually he turned up after delaying us all and parked his car next to the police station. He steamed straight into the pub and we all went for it.

'Then a few pubs later Romano realised he'd left his car keys in the first pub. He was really upset. They couldn't find them in the pub so he had to go to the police station. He said, "Look, I've had a few beers but I need to get into my car to get my stuff." The police had to break a window to get in. Only seconds after the police have smashed his car window for him, another car pulls up and a little old lady gets out and says, "I've just found these car keys on the front." And they were Romano's. He couldn't believe it!'

And of course no tour can be complete without the obligatory confrontation on the hotel stairs. 'The whole hotel was taken up with Lokomotiv players, bar one room which was let to a local. We rolled in in the small hours, trying to be as quiet as a load of drunk blokes can. But then this local bloke comes out of the bedroom and starts ranting and raving. Then he threw a fire extinguisher at our manager Gary. He fell down the stairs with this fire extinguisher clattering after him. Then the hotel manager woke up and amazingly took our side and threw the ranting bloke out and let us stay. So the local was left shivering half-naked outside.'

Although football is not the prime reason for touring, impressionable foreigners can mistake pub sides for the unlikeliest of opponents. In 1989, the Royal Exchange from Bloxwich in the West Midlands played a Gibraltar national side in a game screened live on Spanish television. Apparently, the locals believed they were playing second division Walsall. Must have been those Brummie accents that fooled them, lads.

'We did the whole thing just like the professionals – a minute's silence for Hillsborough, exchanging pennants and crates of beer in the changing rooms afterwards,' said pub landlord David Mason. Sadly, Walsall, aka the Royal Exchange, didn't triumph. The fact that goalkeeper Darren Yarnell was named the man of the match on TV at least compensated for an 8-0 defeat.

Till Dieppe us do part

The club tour is such an awesome event that marriages can be wrecked by it. David Lane of the Windy Millers has some cautionary tales. 'It used to be a standing joke that everyone connected with us split up. The women don't like a group of lads going off and enjoying themselves on tour. One player climbed out of his bedroom window and then phoned from Belgium to tell his girlfriend he'd just popped out for a pint of milk. She'd had the police out looking for him. They split up for six months over that.'

One of the players' wives actually left him after a club tour in Blackpool. The scenario would have made a classic plot for *Whatever Happened to the Likely Lads?*

'He'd had a few drinks and he caught the wrong train home and ended up in London instead of Nuneaton,' explains Lane. 'It was a windy, rainy Saturday night and as the game was off because of a waterlogged pitch, we had a skinful instead. We got split up, and two of the lads decided to take the train to Manchester to go clubbing. They got to Manchester, found a club, but eventually ran out of money. So they decided to spend their last bit of cash on an early-morning train to Nuneaton, but fell asleep on it and found themselves in London on a Sunday morning.'

The tentative phone call that followed was surely the classic scene that Bob and Thelma never filmed. 'This lad had no money left so he had to phone his wife and plead with her to pick him up in the car. At first she said, "Yes, I can pick you up from the station," thinking it was Nuneaton, but then she found out it was London and went mad.'

The couple are now reconciled, although a condition of the wife's return was that her husband gave up playing for the Windy Millers. 'She thought we were the cause of all their problems,' says an indignant Lane. 'Even now he's still too scared to socialise with us.'

And no one will ever forget the day Dick went to Belgium. 'He was about to get married, but the day before he went away he told his fiancée that everything was off. He'd even sold the house. He'd arranged everything so that the tour gave him time to wait for things to cool down at home.'

Football tours can even perpetuate class warfare. Milldean's day trip to Windsor remains an infamous date in the club's annals. The famous playing grounds of Eton have seen nothing like Milldean, a group of Millwall-supporting south Londoners. Barry Knox, the club's secretary at the time, talks us through the day.

'There were about 50 of us on the coach: the players, their wives, girlfriends and kids. We played on Eton's ground and won, but the side we were playing, their ref was cheating by adding on extra time. It was a red-hot day and there were a few heavy tackles on the pitch. After the game they said we couldn't go back to use their showers as we weren't sporting.'

But, as Kipling wrote, 'If you can keep your head when all about you are losing theirs and blaming it on you' . . . Knox used his initiative and asked the landlord of a pub if the players could all go in.

'He said yes, and all the lads walked in in their kit and went straight into the gents with their towels! You'd never seen anything like it. We had a good drink and then went to Windsor for the day. It was like unleashing a load of kids on something they'd never seen before!'

The retired colonels must have thought the revolution had finally arrived. From the Old Kent Road to leafy Windsor was a long journey for most of the Milldean stars, who until then had probably thought that Windsor Castle was a pub. The clear water of the inviting River Thames was just too much of a temptation for the lads. Used to the murkier version at Bermondsey, the day turned into a classic *Only Fools and Horses*-style scenario as the players and their families boozed their way around Windsor.

'Even one of the players' dads stripped down to his underpants and dived in the river,' laughs Knox. 'The kids were saying, "Look, Daddy's jumping off the bridge!" The funniest part was when George Ward, who's now the secretary/manager, lost his diver's watch in twenty feet of water! He'd been proudly showing it off all day. We had to keep diving into that bloody river looking for it, but he never got it back.'

But jumping in the river is not something you should try at home. 'After we'd been jumping in the river this old bloke came up to us and said, "You don't want to be doing that – the kids throw scaffolding poles off the bridge and you'll impale yourself." I thought, thanks. You've been watching us jumping all afternoon,' remembers watch-loser George Ward. 'There were also these water ferries on the river and if you'd mistimed your jump you'd have gone straight through the roof of the bar.'

Other day trips have had a more serious role in fund raising for the club; Milldean has long been going to the dogs. Twice a year Milldean have a night at Catford greyhound-racing track, with the help of the club sponsors. 'The club wouldn't be able to afford to play at our ground if it wasn't for this. We can clear a grand each time,' says Knox. Each player sponsors a dog for a fiver, and several friendly local firms help out by sponsoring each race. 'It keeps the gamblers happy and the women too, as they get a night out.'

As for Milldean's foreign tours, they rarely include football matches, but are great for team spirit. Their first trip was to Lloret ('the Southend of Spain'), but after two local clubs pulled out of games after the Milldean lads had some problems getting out of bed for a fixture, the players had to keep fit by drinking the London Pub out of tequila slammers.

'Everyone behaves like big kids. The only game of football we played was on the lawn in front of the hotel, but we all told our wives we'd got beaten in the final,' says Ward. 'It was seven in the evening and we were all kicking these sprinklers over and the ball kept going in the pool which was freezing. Whoever had to get the ball nearly fainted when they went in the water. They'd get it and then be lying on the grass for half an hour trying to thaw out.'

Like the club's Windsor trip, Milldean's foreign tours have resulted in near fatalities, reveals Ward. 'A lad called Pottsy had been losing at three card brag all day. He had one card left and stood on the balcony three storeys up and said, "Right, if this card doesn't win I'm jumping in the swimming pool the short way!" Thank God he won because the bastard would have jumped!'

In fact, the only thing that can make a football team behave on tour is a TV crew. Milldean made a similar non-footballing excursion to Blackpool when a TV crew was following their season for a documentary shown on Channel 4. This resulted in the only recorded instance of a B & B actually welcoming a football team.

'Everybody behaved themselves, because we were aware of the cameras,' laughs Ward. 'We had a few beers on the train and with typical organisation we'd not booked in anywhere. So we knocked on the door and this bloke saw a football team and said, "No chance." Then we said we've got a film crew with us and he went round the back. He came back a few minutes later and had miraculously found some rooms. He'd put on a leopard-skin shirt and medallion and looked like Del Boy. After that, he couldn't do enough for us.'

How did they ever win the war?

The foreign tour can be rowdy, but you sense that it's better than outright war. Had Genghis Khan and his hordes possessed Polaroids, Vaseline and a detailed fixture list of the bars in Belgium, the history of Europe might have been a lot more peaceful.

The details of the Windy Millers' foreign excursions read like a manual in the art of men behaving badly. There was nearly a terrorist incident when the players brandished water pistols through the Dutch customs. In Holland, one player was tripped up, put in the shower, covered in Vaseline and then daubed with shaving foam just before they were due to go out. The younger players (the Rent Shop Boys) were taunted with a huge carrot. Another player had his bed taken apart and reassembled in the hotel corridor. And there were the inevitable bets on who would be first to throw up and Polaroid snaps of players on the toilet.

Each tour has been given a name in the annals of Windy Millers history, such as the Snake and Fudgepackers tour (a politically incorrect reference to alleged homosexual activity), the Emotional Experience Tour ('Captain Deep met this girl and just sat on the beach staring at the sea for two hours saying it was a very emotional experience'), the Rent Shop Boys Go Dutch tour (the time the youth squad was invited along) and the self-explanatory Hissed and Arseholed tour of Bournemouth. Sometimes they have a collective dress code, such as the orange rave tops which were worn in Holland.

'One of us, Gripper, came in late and what happened to him we don't know,' reminisces keeper Keith 'Fashion Flaw' Jones about one of the trips. 'He'd got one shoe on and just a sock on his other foot. His trousers were on, in a fashion, his shirt had been ripped and was hanging off him, and one arm of his jacket was ripped off. He just walked in and said, "Fuckin' hell, I've had a great time!"'

The only part of his evening that could be pieced together was how he lost his shoe – it was put on the roof of a car after another player spotted him sleeping. The car then moved away as Gripper gave chase, but thinking he was being pursued by an English psychopath, the driver simply sped off.

'Another time in Belgium we knew that a few of us were going to be out late so we had a word with the manager and he gave us a spare key,' continues Jones. 'But Captain Deep didn't know this so we told him that if he wasn't in by two then the manager was going to definitely lock us out. He eventually got in at about half past three and was banging and banging away on the door for 45 minutes, without realising that it was actually open!'

But the mother of all bad taste tour stories is surely the time Mr Spoons drank a bottle of Southern Comfort on the way to Holland.

'Mr Spoons was a real Norman No Mates character, also known as Captain Wobbly and Jarhead,' explains a source close to the club. 'He bought this bottle of Southern Comfort as we left Nuneaton. We were all asking him for a drink of it but he kept saying, "It's mine," and he wouldn't let us have a drop. So when he went down the back of the coach we got hold of it, undid it, and finished most of it.'

'We left just enough Southern Comfort in so it would still taste like the real thing and then filled it with piss. Then we put some tape over the top so he wouldn't realise it was tampered with. And he drank the lot! He was so drunk he didn't notice. We were going, "Down in one!" – and he drank it! He just said, "It's lovely, but it's a bit warm . . ." We were killing ourselves and we didn't have the heart to tell him what had happened. His missus wouldn't kiss him for months after she found out. We all felt a bit guilty afterwards. And although you're laughing you wonder when it might have happened to you . . .'

Were Hieronymous Bosch, whoever he played for, alive today, he would find infinite material for his hellish artistic visions on the club tour. And should John Cleese and Connie Booth ever make another series of *Fawlty Towers* then the great unwritten episode would surely involve a Sunday league football team invading Torquay.

In it Basil would confront fifteen drunken footballers sneaking in at three in the morning after a session at a dodgy disco followed by a late-night kebab in Torquay. He suspects the goalkeeper of molesting Polly and is incensed that Sybil actually seems to like them, claiming they need the money from the bulk booking. Manuel has been caught falling through the hedge in his Barcelona shirt after having a midnight kickabout on the hotel lawn with the drunken footballers, while the chef is plastered in the bar with Captain Deep and the Major.

Basil turns to Sybil and declares, 'Ha, the rubbish we get in here!' before deciding to throw this 'bunch of arse' out on the spot. That is, until he's consoled by the team captain offering him a bottle of Southern Comfort.

But perhaps this end-of-season mayhem is understandable when you consider the footballer's newfound status. These players are role models in the public bar and the strain of a season under media scrutiny from the club programme compiler is massive. Following the Bosman ruling, Sunday league players are now free to demand a market price for their services, so we should not be surprised if a jug of beer for every hat-trick sometimes goes to their heads. Faced with adulation and feted like pop stars by the club's fan (and his dog), it is inevitable that some should be tempted by drink, drugs or women – or all three on a good night.

After the club tour, the lads will have a few weeks off before pre-season training in the pub starts again and the first friendly results in the first punch-up and sendings-off of the new season. Throughout the summer they will have been as miserable as Morrissey. Life is not complete for them without the reassuring thud of leather on gut. Even the malfunctioning showers seem inviting. Any lay-off is too long, but soon the answerphone message will come from a harassed secretary and it will be time to put on the unwashed boots and welcome another Sunday muddy Sunday.

Other sport titles published by Virgin:

FOOTBALL BABYLON 2

by

Russ Williams

In the tradition of the infamous *Football Babylon* we bring you *Football Babylon 2* – the lurid truth behind the glossy face of world football.

The first book to tackle the issues that really matter, to uncover the truth behind the rumours, to examine the myths and expose the corruption. From death on the fields to sex in the dressing room, from plagues of locusts to voodoo curses, Russ Williams has uncovered it all.

Published in paperback at £7.99 and available at all good bookshops or from Virgin Publishing on 0171-386 3300.

ISBN 0 7535 0211 9

FA CARLING PREMIERSHIP POCKET ANNUAL 1998–1999

by

Bruce Smith

Now in its sixth year and more than ever an unparalleled and indispensible source of facts, figures and stats on the Premier League. Providing a guide to the season for every club and every player in the Premiership, it is an essential companion to the whole of the 1998–99 season in a handy pocket-size.

With a full club-directory, detailed, up-to-the-minute fixture list and full reviews of clubs, players and managers, The *Virgin FA Carling Premiership Annual* is the only way to get the most out of the new season.

Published in paperback at £4.99 and available at all good bookshops or from Virgin Publishing on 0171-386 3300.

ISBN 0 7535 0212 7

THE FOOTBALL LEAGUE POCKET ANNUAL 1998–1999

by

Bruce Smith

The *Virgin Football League Pocket Annual 1998–99* is your essential guide to the football league season and includes all the information you could possibly need. It is an unparalleled and indispensible source of facts, figures and stats in a handy pocket-size. Providing a guide to the season for every club and every player in the Football League.

- Includes all FA Cup and League Cup matches and fixtures
- Comprehensive and unique records including past league tables and scorers
- Full fixture lists for 1998-99
- All Football League, FA Cup, League Cup and European results from 1997–98
- Player A-Z, covering every squad member, with a full statistical round up
- Lists all current managers and their managerial records

Published in paperback at £4.99 and available at all good bookshops or from Virgin Publishing on 0171-386 3300.

ISBN 0 7535 0217 8

THE RUGBY UNION POCKET ANNUAL 1998–1999

by

Bruce Smith

With a full club-directory, and a special focus on the top two divisions, detailed, up-to-the-minute fixture list and full reviews of clubs and players, The *Virgin Rugby Union Pocket Annual* is your best guide to the season.

- Includes all league and cup competitions in England, Ireland, Scotland and Wales
- Comprehensive and unique records including past tables
- Full fixture lists for 1998–99
- All the results from 1997–98
- Player A–Z, covering every squad member, with a full statistical round up
- Five nations Championship 1998 round-up and statistics, plus all other international matches

Published in paperback at £4.99 and available at all good bookshops or from Virgin Publishing on 0171-386 3300.

ISBN 0 7535 0237 2

GOALKEEPERS ARE DIFFERENT

by

Brian Glanville

"The Great Football Novel has been written."
When Saturday Comes

A fascinating glimpse into the world of a professional footballer –
in the person of Ronnie Blake, a rising young goalkeeper, from his
early days as a club apprentice to the exhilarating heights at the
top of the tree.

Ronnie's story offers a real insight into the highs and lows of
football – the misery of injury and rejection, the exhilaration of
signing schoolboy forms and making it into the first team, but most
exciting of all the tremendous thrill of running out on to the pitch
in front of a roaring crowd, perhaps even in the Cup final at
Wembley.

Published in paperback at £6.99 and available at all good
bookshops or from Virgin Publishing on 0171-386 3300.

ISBN 0 7535 0243 7